NORTH JERSEY
LEGACIES

NORTH JERSEY LEGACIES

Hidden History from the Gateway to the Skylands

Gordon Bond

Charleston THE London
History
PRESS

Published by The History Press
Charleston, SC 29403
www.historypress.net

Front cover design by Gordon Bond. Images: locomotive image, *Gordon Bond*; Thomas
Mundy Peterson, *Perth Amboy Public Library*; dog Laika, *Tass/Sovfoto*; Newark Airport, *Joseph
Bond*; "Join or Die," *Wikipedia*; Lee Theatre, *Fort Lee Film Commission*; Dust Bowl, *NOAA George
E. Marsh Album, taken at Stratford, Texas, April 18, 1935.*
Back cover: John Bull on display at the World Columbian Exposition in Chicago, 1893.

First published 2012

Manufactured in the United States

ISBN 978.1.60949.556.5

Library of Congress Cataloging-in-Publication Data

Bond, Gordon.
North Jersey legacies : hidden history from the Gateway to the Skylands / Gordon Bond.
p. cm.
Includes bibliographical references.
ISBN 978-1-60949-556-5
1. New Jersey--History, Local. 2. New Jersey--History. 3. New Jersey--Biography. I. Title.
F134.6.B66 2012
974.9--dc23
2012002409

Notice: The information in this book is true and complete to the best of our knowledge. It is
offered without guarantee on the part of the author or The History Press. The author and
The History Press disclaim all liability in connection with the use of this book.

For Zooey.

Contents

Introduction and Acknowledgements

This book is the result of an occupational hazard. In the fall of 2008, I started www.GardenStateLegacy.com, an online quarterly magazine devoted to New Jersey history. And now I can't read about history or watch a documentary about history without being "on alert" for a New Jersey connection—*any* New Jersey connection.

I am often struck by just how many times I actually find one. The Garden State features to some degree—even as a footnote—in larger historical stories far more often than one might think. It could just be a matter of someone from the state going on to something of historic importance somewhere else or that by dumb luck something just happened to occur within its borders. But as a New Jersey native and resident, even the thinnest link resonates with my sense of identity—and my seemingly never-ending quest for material for the magazine.

What follows is a collection of five articles I have written for GSL plus two new pieces specifically for this book, each about people and events that, by happenstance, connected the Garden State to the broader historic events of the nation and even the world. How I came upon these subjects is an interesting enough back story—and gives credit to some unwitting inspirations.

When I began GSL, I had a day job that required a commute of an hour or more each way, driving along Route 22 at rush hour. To help pass the tedious time stuck in traffic, I started listening to books on CD. Among these was Timothy Egan's excellent account of the Dust Bowl, *The Worst*

Hard Time. Driving home one day, I listened to a section about a dust storm that became so great that it reached from the Midwest to the East Coast. That meant New Jersey must have also had a taste of what those out on the prairies were suffering. What I didn't expect was that it got this far twice, and the second time with a truly melodramatic flair that changed history.

Inspiration struck again during a similar bid to beat rush hour boredom. I was listening to *The Life and Times of the Thunderbolt Kid*, a reminiscence of growing up in the America of the 1950s by another favorite author of mine, Bill Bryson. In passing, he mentioned a supposed experiment in subliminal advertising conducted in a Fort Lee, New Jersey movie theater. From that single sentence grew a new line of research into an obscure yet fascinating tidbit of Garden State history. My thanks to Mr. Bryson, and also George Parker for helping proof the chapter and Lou Azzolini for the photo of the theater where the alleged experiment took place.

Often, one line of research leads to other unexpected areas. As I write this, I am also researching a book about New Jersey's deadliest train wreck on February 6, 1951, in Woodbridge, when the Pennsylvania Railroad's express commuter train, the Broker, careened from the embankment, killing eighty-five and injuring hundreds more. Immersing myself in early twentieth-century railroading, I picked up a bundled collection of random rail fan magazines at an antique shop. Among the articles was one about experiments the Pennsylvania Railroad was conducting with a new form of communication on a northeast New Jersey branch line. I had never given it much thought, but considering trains have been operating longer than there has been technology like radio, how *did* an engineer up front talk to the conductor in the caboose? What that article didn't mention, however, and what my research turned up, was the tragic accident and political pressures that led to these critical experiments on a New Jersey rail line. Thank you to Mike Carter for allowing me to use a classic photo showing the communications equipment on a locomotive.

Sometimes history is sitting next to us in the shape of our family and friends—often, only appreciated after the person is gone. Such was the case with George Chaplenko. I had known him casually when we both belonged to the same amateur astronomy club—a chain-smoking elderly man, often clad in loud check jackets and a baseball cap, with a thick Ukrainian accent and a warm smile. I had heard anecdotes of his life—of his conscription into the Russian army and time spent in a German prisoner of war camp during the Second World War and his subsequent career in engineering with several patents to his name. Also, that he had been the first American to hear the news that the Soviets had launched Sputnik 2 as he listened in on a shortwave radio from Perth Amboy, New Jersey. Unfortunately, George passed away before I began writing seriously, but thanks to longtime fellow Amateur Astronomers, Inc. members Alan and Bonnie Witzgall, I was able to put the story together.

This isn't my first book. In 2010, I published *James Parker: A Printer on the Eve of Revolution*, an in-depth biography of the man who established New Jersey's first permanent print shop. Parker's life and career were directly impacted by the events that heralded the twilight of the British Empire in North America. Among the events to fatally strain the bonds between England and the colonies was the 1765 Stamp Act. Before it was even to take effect, it was met by passionate protest and outright violence. Throughout New York there began to appear what historians consider the most virulent anti–Stamp Act publication, in the style of a newspaper. The incensed local government wanted to know who would dare write such things—and who would dare print it? Was New Jersey's James Parker involved? It may all depend on the interpretation of a single word.

If you're a longtime GSL subscriber who has already read these articles, I've written two new chapters just for this book—consider them literary "bonus tracks." When you think of the history of aviation, New Jersey probably doesn't leap to mind. Yet while it may have been born in North Carolina, aviation matured into an industry in the Garden State—specifically at what is today Newark Liberty Airport. My thanks to Ray Shapp, a retired airline pilot, who not only proofread the chapter, but also added some important information. Thanks also go to Tom Ankner, George Hawley, PhD, and Timothy Lewis at the Newark Public Library; John Beekman of the Jersey City Free Public Library's New Jersey Room; and Joseph Bond for providing many of the photos. Thanks also to Alan P. Witzgall for scanning the slides.

The other new chapter is very much in the theme of how fate conspired for history to happen in New Jersey. By dumb luck, the first election following passage of the Fifteenth Amendment to the U.S. Constitution just happened to occur at Perth Amboy. Yet the story of how Thomas Peterson became the first African American to vote under this amendment and what he did with that unexpected honor is a fascinating study in the complexities of race relations in post–Civil War New Jersey. I'd like to thank Bill Pavlovsky for helping proof this chapter and John Dyke for some excellent and rare illustrations. My sincere thanks to the Perth Amboy Free Public Library for allowing me to scan Mr. Peterson's photograph.

Thank you to Matt Dowling for permission to reprint from the *Trenton Evening Times* newspaper.

My thanks to Whitney Tarella for putting up with my many emails; my copyeditor, Darcy Mahan; and everyone at The History Press for turning this collection into a book.

Thank you to my parents, Jacqueline and Joseph Bond, for their love and support.

But my greatest debt of gratitude must be reserved for my wife, Stephanie M. Hoagland, for her patient support of my crazy dream of being a history writer when I grow up.

New Jersey may be a footnote in these tangential tales, but they are the kind of unexpected connections that make exploring New Jersey's history so delightful.

CHAPTER 1

Dust in the Garden

The Days the Dust Bowl Came to the Garden State

O n May 11, 1934, Dr. Robert C. Clothier, president of Rutgers University, announced a year's leave of absence for his dean of the College of Agriculture, Dr. Jacob G. Lipman. Beginning on July 1, Dr. Lipman was to direct a vast effort by the U.S. Department of Agriculture to inventory soil fertility for the entire United States.

But beneath that drearily academic-sounding appointment was a dire desperation. The government knew something had gone terribly wrong with the land, and they needed this Russian immigrant and men like him. Lipman had earned a reputation as one of the world's foremost soil scientists, having received his BS from Rutgers in 1898 and a PhD in agricultural chemistry from Cornell in 1903. Though he was still working on the degree at Cornell, Rutgers thought enough of his work to have tapped him to develop its new agricultural program in 1901.

Whether you made your living from the land or just grew a couple of tomato plants in your backyard, the importance of the quality of the dirt was long understood. Yet it was Lipman who elevated it from an anecdotal art into a vital science. Indeed, his career had been dedicated to establishing soil science as a discipline. In 1916, he founded a periodical, the appropriately named *Soil Science*, which had become internationally recognized as the journal of record for the field.

According to the announcement that appeared in the *Daily Home News*, the task he was to undertake that July was "[o]ne of the largest projects ever undertaken in the field of soil science, the major objective of the inventory will be to provide a new and more accurate basis for determining national

Men like Rutgers University's Dr. Jacob G. Lipman worked to establish the discipline of soil science in the face of the ecological disaster of the Dust Bowl.

policies for use of land for agriculture, forests, recreation and other purposes and to point the way to a more effective conservation of the plant food resources of soil."

Given the grim news coming from the American heartland, it would not be hyperbole to say that the fate of the United States itself rested on the success or failure of such undertakings. Lipman and his colleagues were given the task of shaping federal government policy regarding the use of the land.

And, hopefully, to steer us out of the worst ecological disaster of the twentieth century.

HOMESTEAD

The story of the Dust Bowl reads like the quintessential American tragedy. Indeed, it was creative fodder for the classic books (and later movies) *The Grapes of Wrath* and *Of Mice and Men* by John Steinbeck. But its roots are buried in even deeper aspects of the American mythos.

Right from the start, even before the American Revolution, those who sought to command the resources of the New World used promises of land to lure would-be settlers. The agricultural utopia envisioned by Thomas

Jefferson was based on his noble yeoman farmer concept. Despite the rise of Hamiltonian market paradigms, the post-Revolutionary United States was still largely a rural place well into the nineteenth century.

As early as the 1840s, there was a push by Jacksonian Democrats to officially codify the means by which a new generation of settlers would be encouraged to fulfill what many saw as America's Manifest Destiny. The Preemption Act of 1841 permitted squatters on government land who were heads of households, widows, single men over twenty-one (so long as they were citizens or intended to become naturalized) and who had lived there for at least fourteen months to purchase up to 160 acres at the low price of $1.25 per acre before the land was offered for sale to the public. The states of Ohio, Indiana, Illinois, Alabama, Missouri, Mississippi, Louisiana, Arkansas and Michigan were admitted to the Union as a result, and settlers made use of this act in the Kansas and Nebraska Territories, which were opened to settlement in 1854.

By the 1850s, the concept had evolved into the Homestead Act. Passage was delayed by the fears of southern states of new competition to their plantation system, but once they seceded during the Civil War, their objections were a moot point. Pushed by the radical reformer George H. Evans and publisher Horace Greeley ("Go West, young man, go West and grow up with the country"), it was signed into law by President Abraham Lincoln on May 20, 1862. It gave applicants freehold title to between 160 and 640 acres of undeveloped land outside of the original thirteen colonies. The process was simple enough—file an application, improve the land and file for deed of title. Even freed slaves could apply.

And so they came. Wave after wave.

It was the classic American story—hardy settlers, seeking a better life for themselves and their families. True, the work was hard, but it was honest. The prairies, with their seemingly endless acres of fertile soil and big skies, offered up opportunity to any man who was willing to put his back into his living.

DROUGHT

In its simplest terms, the cause of the Dust Bowl was drought. But serious dry periods were nothing new in the hundreds of thousands of years of natural history on the semiarid North American High Plains. They are balanced by wet spells, and it is this alternating of dry and wet periods—and even the occasional wildfire—that supported the shortgrass prairie biome that evolved to thrive there. The root systems of these grasses held the soil and moisture in place in the face of the high winds that are the norm. The grasses were the key.

To farmers and cattlemen, however, such grasses were in the way. They cleared the land to make way for the wheat and grain that could fetch a good price or feed livestock. Perhaps, it has been argued, larger farming interests might have been able to employ smarter long-term cultivation practices. But such approaches weren't always efficient for the kinds of small farmers lured by the promises of the Homestead Act. They were further encouraged by the bounty brought on by an unusually prolonged wet period in the 1920s and the hyper-demand for grain exports to Europe during the First World War. The amount of land under cultivation tripled between 1925 and 1930 alone. Migration west was further driven by the crash of Wall Street in October 1929. Fleeing the increasingly acute effects of the Great Depression, families hungry for work fled west.

The last ingredient in this perfect ecological storm came the following year as the pendulum swung back yet again and the droughts started once more in earnest. They easily killed the crops introduced by farmers that were ill suited to the change. And this time there were no grasses to hold the fine topsoil in place against the wind.

"SOME REALLY SERIOUS THINKING"

To the residents of New Jersey, the prairies were a world away. In 1934, the railroads were still the primary means of reaching the interior of the country and could take days. Airplanes were still something of a novelty, and rural roads were abysmal. Though in its waning days, the West was still wild, and cowboys still drove herds across the plains. The American Midwest was still a remote, abstract, almost exotic concept for those "back east."

Nevertheless, newspapers and newsreels gave a hint that something had gone wrong out there. Terribly wrong. On May 11, 1934, the *New York Times* ran a front-page article telling of a bleak forecast for the winter wheat—a gauge of the real damage being done and its implications for the nation as a whole. The U.S. Department of Agriculture predicted a yield of 461,471,000 bushels—over 30,000,000 bushels fewer than the ten-year average. "Today's crop report took no account of the increasing severity of the drought during the past ten days," the story warned, "during which the rainfall throughout the principal wheat-growing sections has been less than a fourth of normal." Indeed, it was the driest season on record since 1885.

The next day, the Friday evening edition of the *Elizabeth Daily Journal* for May 11, 1934, reported that "[a]pprehension over middle America's crop prospects grew hourly" in the face of a huge dust storm that had descended on Chicago and seemed to be continuing east. The administration of Franklin D. Roosevelt attempted to calm fears of famine—something Europe had seen recently, making it a very real and primal fear. They "asserted there still should be enough food to go around." But Agriculture secretary Henry A. Wallace was quoted saying that while "[t]here is certainly no immediate danger of food shortage of any kind in this country…if this drought continues, it behooves all of us to do some really serious thinking."

There was something almost biblical about the stories coming out of the nation's interior. Drought and the vague fear of famine were only the half of it. Vast dust storms—"black blizzards"—were swallowing whole towns, choking out entire herds of livestock and even derailing trains. It was easy to perhaps dismiss such claims as exaggerations.

Sure, things were bad out there—but could they really be *that* bad?

Then, on May 9, 1934, out on the northern prairies of the Dakotas and Montana, the winds began to march east, drawing up the land. Building, broiling, reaching for the jet stream, several whirlwinds merged into one huge mass. By the time it rolled into Illinois and Ohio the next day, amazed pilots

Arthur Rothstein's classic photo of a farmer and sons walking in the face of a dust storm in Cimarron County, Oklahoma, helped to prove the reality of the suffering of those in the Midwest during the Dust Bowl.

trying to outrun the dust were forced to strain their prop-driven airplanes to their uppermost limits, topping out at around fifteen thousand feet—and still they were unable to escape its apocalyptic grasp. It was estimated that this one dust storm transported three tons of dust for every American alive that day.

It was nothing less than the greatest American dust storm on record.

Chicago was the first major urban center to get dumped on—some six thousand tons of prairie fell that night. As the sun rose, Scranton, Pennsylvania, Boston and New York found the once bright, clear day choked away as dust fell like snow.

The front-page headline of the May 11, 1934 edition of the *Trenton Evening Times* read, "Trenton Sees Effects of Western Dust Blizzard." The sky over the state's capital had "a yellowish, mud-like hue."

The next day, the *Asbury Park Evening Press* featured a photo of an obscured New York skyline under the headline "Clouds of Dust from West Cast Pall Over Seaboard."

"Clouds of dust, thousands of feet high," the article read, "which arose in the parched fields of the Northwest as far off as Montana cast a gloomy pall over the shore yesterday and filtered the rays of the sun in a half-light similar to that of a partial eclipse of the sun."

On May 11, 1934, the *Trenton Evening Times* reported how the sky over the state's capital took on "a yellowish, mud-like hue." *Courtesy of the* Times of Trenton.

It was estimated that "300,000,000 tons of what used to be topsoil in the Mississippi and Missouri river valleys had been swept aloft by a strong northeast wind and liberally sprinkled over half of the country."

New Jersey seems to have been luckier than its neighbor across the Hudson. "Locally, residents were fortunate in that the dust rode high," the *Asbury Park Evening Press* continued. "Very little irritation was caused and the phenomena was looked on rather as a nuisance. In New York, the dust settled somewhat and annoyed people with throat afflictions." Indeed, they made a point of noting that the dust "will not materially effect [*sic*] a weekend of fair and cooler weather."

The *New York Times* headline, however, read: "Huge Dust Cloud, Blown 1,500 Miles, Dims City 5 Hours."

In Manhattan, streetlights came on, and tourists on the observation deck of the Empire State Building were met not by the normally breathtaking view but rather a literally breathtaking wall of dust. Below, life ground to an astonished halt. It was estimated that only 50 percent of the normal amount of sunlight fell into the city.

As Timothy Egan, author of the book *The Worst Hard Time*, pointed out, New York in 1934 was a dirty place to begin with. An average day saw dust measured at 227 parts per square millimeter—in other words, enough to bother people with health problems. The day the dust fell, however, the readings were 619 parts per square millimeter at the height of the storm. Doctors' offices and hospitals were clogged by sputtering, coughing New Yorkers seeking something to clear their lungs and soothe irritated eyes. NBC radio changed its studio air filters hourly.

At its height, the storm covered some 1,800 miles wide, reaching from the Great Plains right out into the Atlantic Ocean. The captain of the cargo ship *Deutschland*, seeing the billowing clouds obscuring the skyline, delayed coming into port, unsure what catastrophe had befallen the city.

If anyone in the metropolis doubted the magnitude of the crisis out in the faraway world of the homesteaders, here it now was, in a thick coating, quite literally on their doorsteps.

"Something Had Gone Wrong with the Land"

Dr. James H. Kimble of the National Weather Bureau told the *New York Times*, "The explanation of the dust cloud is simple. The surface soil in the upper Missouri and Mississippi Valleys was fine and loose as a result of the drought. All that was needed was a persistent and direct wind."

The human factor in the tragedy had yet to be accepted for a number of reasons. One was inherent in the character of the people who would even consider chancing their hands at a High Plains farm. It takes a fierce independence and hardheaded bravado to take on such a challenge. These were people who didn't take kindly to being told what to do with their land—land that *they* worked with *their* blood, sweat and tears. They took pride in their obstinacy. They were Americans who, like the first settlers and pioneers, didn't give up easily in the face of adversity. Let the winds howl. They'd just dig in, hold on and growl right back! Under the right circumstances, such spirit would be laudable. In 1934, however, it was a hubris that was killing them.

Some who had made a study of the soil understood the severity of the situation and saw a potential solution. They could see that the real cause of all this misery was human misuse of the land. It wasn't that the farmers were bad people. Most simply didn't know better—a combination of pride and ignorance. What was needed was to inspire a wholesale change in their attitudes and practices.

The land, however, was breaking hardened men. Unable to withstand the hardships on themselves and their families, they packed their belongings into cars and turned their backs on the prairies. Those who remained began to understand that they couldn't survive without help—they needed the guidance of smart men, like Dr. Lipman from Rutgers, to help them salvage their own livelihoods.

Like Lipman, Hugh Hammond Bennett spent his career advocating for soil conservation. Born near Wadesboro in Anson County, North Carolina, and graduating from the University of North Carolina in 1903, Bennett became a soil surveyor, conducting studies in the United States and abroad. What he saw convinced him that soil erosion was a serious problem facing the planet as a whole. He would advocate soil conservation in articles appearing everywhere from scientific journals to *Country Gentleman* magazine. In 1933, when the Soil Erosion Service was established as part of the United States Department of the Interior, Bennett was the obvious choice as director. He would become the strongest voice in the Roosevelt administration to assert that an entirely new agricultural policy was the only thing that could save the day.

The Dust Bowl would visit the East Coast one more time, in a fashion worthy of a Hollywood movie. On April 19, 1935, Bennett walked into Room 333 of the Senate Office Building in Washington, D.C., to try and sell his schemes for what amounted to an ecological "New Deal." Rather than quitting the land, farmers would be encouraged to become part of the solution by building natural barriers to the spread of dunes, creating man-made lakes and holding tanks for water and forming community farms following strict soil conservation practices. He had been given $5 million in federal money to fund his Soil Erosion Service in 1933, but he saw a more permanent future for it.

Obviously, the small taste New Jersey and the East Coast had of the dust was nothing when compared with the suffering of those in the thick of it. But it was enough to help make Bennett's point. "When people along the eastern seaboard began to taste fresh soil from the plains two thousand miles away," he said, "many of them realized for the first time that somewhere, something had gone wrong with the land."

As he settled into his presentation in 1935, with his charts and maps, many senators' eyes glazed over. He was losing them.

Then, an aide whispered something in his ear.

He began to digress and stall, repeating facts, reminiscing about farming techniques learned on his daddy's North Carolina farm. And then, as if on cue, though midday, it began to get dark outside. Really dark. Yet another massive dust storm had caught the jet stream to the East Coast.

"*This*, gentlemen, is what I'm talking about," Bennett told the startled senators. Pointing out the window, he declared, "There goes Oklahoma!"

Within a day, Bennett had funding to make his Soil Erosion Service a permanent fixture of the United States government—one he would head until his retirement in 1951. On April 27, 1935, the soil conservation act passed.

The healing could begin.

Garden State Legacy #2, December 2008

CHAPTER 2

1/3,000th of a Second in Fort Lee

A Mysterious Experiment in Subliminal Advertising

America approached the middle of the twentieth century with a sort of swagger. We had, after all, just made the world safe for democracy from the Fascists of Europe and Asia. Where the ravages of war had lain waste to much of their economies, industries and infrastructure, American factories were intact. They just switched from wartime production to cranking out the goods demanded by the pent-up consumerism of a nation eager to get on with lives the war had put on hold. Sure, "Uncle Joe" Stalin and his red minions were kicking up a fuss in Berlin, and Communist China threatened to weigh in on the side of North Korea's attempt to "reunite" the peninsula. But we were flush with our successes as we strutted onto the world stage as the superpower we always suspected we really were.

To a significant demographic (i.e., Caucasian) who grew up back then, the 1950s were a sort of golden era. Economically, we were strong. Our industry and technology seemed to stand up to the best the Russians had to offer. Indeed, American science and technology seemed both the cause and cure for all our ills. Our cars were roomy and powerful. Rosie the Riveter was being lured back into her kitchen by gleaming new appliances that offered to make life in the Western Hemisphere much easier. American TVs flickered in living rooms as families settled down to their modern—futuristic, even—pre-packaged "TV dinners."

The "Atomic Age" perhaps best exemplified the proverbial double-edged sword of technology. Optimistic futurists envisioned atomic rockets launching humanity into a new age of discovery in outer space or atomic reactors that would soon be harnessing the power of the sun to meet the world's energy needs for generations to come. The U.S. Food and Drug Administration approved its first radiopharmaceutical—sodium iodide 1-131 for thyroid patients—in 1951, furthering the field of "nuclear medicine."

Yet at the same time, with the rise of a nuclear arms race with the USSR, these visions of a brave new atomic world were simultaneously tempered by the very real possibility of nuclear inhalation.

Still, it seemed like there wasn't any problem, large or small, that couldn't ultimately be conquered by American technological prowess. Science (married to technology) was exemplified as both scourge and savior in a strange experiment said to have been conducted in a darkened movie theater in Fort Lee, New Jersey.

DELVING INTO THE MIND

The ability of medical science to fix the human body has always held out the Promethean promise of also fixing the human mind. Everything from the discredited phrenology that reads a person's character from the bumps on his head to Sigmund Freud's psychoanalysis to John Larson's application of the polygraph in police investigations—all aimed to understand our brains to correct for perceived defects.

And why not? Wouldn't society be a better place if we could heal mental illness or identify the criminal before the crime?

As with many applications of science and technology, however, there is a downside. We are left to balance the benefits against the ethical dilemmas. Consider, for example, the advent of the automobile. It has, at the same time, given us both the auto accident and the ability to speed the injured to help via the ambulance. Delving into the mind carries a host of unique ethical questions. By whose measure, for instance, do we define "normal"? There have been examples in totalitarian states where opposition to a leader's philosophy has been considered a sign of madness. In our own country, polygraphs were employed not only to root out suspected communists but also homosexuals in the so-called "Purple Scare."

Sometimes, however, such exploitation of science had less to do with ideology than with the almighty dollar. If science could be used to understand what made someone a communist or a murderer, couldn't it also be used to discover why someone was attracted to one brand over another?

This was the kind of question that intrigued James Vicary.

VICARY

Born on April 30, 1915, in Detroit, Vicary became fascinated from an early age with understanding what motivated people. While a fifteen-year-old copy boy for the *Detroit Free Press*, he was tasked with conducting a political straw poll that turned out to be correct within 0.06 of 1 percent. He was a restless youth, bouncing between the Henry Ford Trade School, the Civilian Conservation Corps and even hopping freight trains around the country. But he was bright, and his godfather helped finance his education at the University of Michigan, where he earned an AB in 1940. At college, he tried studying art and biology before focusing on sociology. Understanding people's motivations, however, remained at the heart of his interests. In 1937, he organized the university's Bureau of Student Opinion. After graduation, he worked for J.L. Hudson Company, a large Detroit department store, on operations and merchandising.

Vicary declared himself a conscientious objector during World War II but was drafted anyway in 1941 and assigned for two years to the Civilian Public Service in Wellston, Michigan. In 1944, he worked in Princeton, New Jersey, for a polling affiliate of the Gallup Organization, Benson and Benson, conducting surveys on readership, marketing and elections. After a short stint with Crowell-Collier Publishing Company in its research department, he started up his own company, the James M. Vicary Company.

Though described as handsome enough to have walked out of a men's clothing ad, Vicary wasn't the most charismatic of men. But what he lacked in personality, he made up for with dogged determination and managed to present a smoothness to the world.

His company had a rough start, and by 1948, he had to seek employment with the ad agency Benton and Bowles, Inc., as head of advertising copy research, where he tested and modernized its approach to ad copy. By 1950, however, the stress began to get to him—it was rough on the ulcers, he would say—and he left on good terms to return to his own business and independent consulting.

He began publishing his research in both leading trade journals and popular periodicals and speaking at trade conventions. He built a reputation as an articulate source for reporters who were looking for a talking head to cover the latest in the advertising arts. His clients became more impressive as well, including *TIME* magazine, Ford Motor Company, General Mills, B.F. Goodrich and Colgate-Palmolive.

He pioneered the use of something called "eye-blink analysis" as a gauge of a person's emotional stress in response to various stimuli. In short, this looks to the rate at which people blink their eyes—a subconscious act—as an indication of their emotional state. Even recently, this controversial technique has been studied to help detect someone telling a lie. Kuosuke Fukuda of Japan, for example, published a paper, "Eye Blinks: New Indices for the Detection of Deception," in the *International Journal of Psychophysiology* in 2001.

Vicary was also interested in the motivations behind impulse buying. Retailers use our desire for instant gratification to tempt us every day. You go to the supermarket for a loaf of bread, for example, but end up also buying that inexpensive candy bar strategically displayed at the checkout. Your normal, logical line of reasoning—"I'm out of bread and need it to make a sandwich so I'm just buying what I need"—is disrupted by an irrational desire for self-gratification—"Some chocolate would sure taste good right now!"

Another area of pioneering study was word association. In April 1950, the trade journal *Printer's Ink* published Vicary's seminal article on the subject, "How Psychiatric Methods Can Be Applied to Market Research." He claimed to have found that young, newly married housewives found the butcher counter intimidating—they suffered from a sense of inferiority because they were not up on the lingo when it came to different cuts of meat. He recommended butchers be taught how to better interact with their young female customers and use words that would build up their confidence.

Psychologists will sometimes play a word association game with their patients—they say a word and the patient is supposed to say the first word that pops into his head. The chosen word, some claim, is a clue as to what's going on in one's subconscious—showing how they associate words or concepts to one another. Others are more skeptical and consider it little more than a party game.

The implications for marketing and advertising, however, seemed a little more obvious—certain words can trigger a positive response in consumers to a particular product or message. There's a reason words like "sale" or "free" are emphasized. People obviously equate the word "sale" with bargains, and while there may not be such a thing as the proverbial free lunch, the word still catches one's attention. Telling someone it is a "limited offer" imparts an exclusivity that appeals to vanity—"I'm one of only a few people getting this offer so I must be special!"—and a sense of urgency—"If I don't jump on this deal now, it may be gone tomorrow and I'd miss an opportunity!"

Consumers always want to think they are getting a good deal, that they are smart for finding it and that the product will make them cooler, sexier people—even if they know deep down that it won't. But the idea may persuade someone to select one product over another, and advertisers intentionally use words or phrases that will appeal to those inner desires.

Vicary studied people's reactions to the word "lagered" for a brewing company and found that while a third of his test subjects associated the term with "beer," an equal number found it brought to mind such notions as tiredness or dizziness—not the kinds of associations a brewery would want for its products! Needless to say, it didn't use the term.

"A New Morality of Consumption"

The notion of stimulating the unconscious to alter opinion dates back at least to the mixed results of experiments in the mid–1800s but really came into its own in postwar America. Fears of an economic depression were inspired by the idea of hundreds of thousands of GIs returning home and looking for work when the artificially inflated wartime industry would be scaling down. Instead, they brought home a hunger for consumer goods and the desire to start families and were returning to an America sick of rationing and austerity measures. The GI Bill provided many with the financial and educational means to indulge these desires. The increase in demand-side economics boosted the supply-side, generating what many still view as the golden era of modern capitalism.

Another generator of postwar prosperity was advertising, as the push was on to transform wartime thrift into, as author Kelly B. Crandall put it, "a new morality of consumption." Meager living and eschewing personal pleasures to buy war bonds had been propagandized as acts of patriotism, and it was up to a new and more sophisticated approach to advertising to shift Americans into believing spending was now what was good for the country.

Concepts such as "planned obsolescence"—intentionally designing goods with a finite life span to require new purchases later—gave rise to a "keeping up with the Joneses" mentality. Advertising to promote consumerism took on new importance, and psychological concepts were incorporated into these strategies. Ernest Dichter is considered the father of something called "motivational research." Its roots in Freudian psychology are betrayed by Dichter's 1939 study for Chrysler Corporation that linked convertibles with mistresses and sedans with wives.

1/3,000TH of a Second in Fort Lee

But fear of totalitarianism and authoritarian regimes was also part of the postwar landscape for Americans. They had just witnessed the horrible extremes of such societies in the Nazi death camps in Europe and fanatical self-sacrifice of the kamikaze in the Pacific. Lock-stepped Communist troops in the USSR were making us nervous for the future.

While there was a rationale to encouraging people to spend, there was something unsettling about these efforts to control people's thought processes—it smacked too much of the sinister tactics employed in the authoritarian states we feared.

It was against this backdrop that on September 12, 1957, in a New York film studio, Vicary stepped before a cadre of American and British reporters to announce the formation of Subliminal Projection Company, Inc. with Rene Bras and Francis Thayer (the president of the new company).

The company was founded on the results obtained, Vicary claimed, from an experiment they had conducted at a movie theater in Fort Lee, New Jersey. According to a front-page report in the *Wall Street Journal*—this was considered that big of a news item—"several close-mouthed men walked into a New Jersey motion picture house and fitted a strange mechanism to the film projector."

Theatergoers had settled in to watch *The Picnic*, a 1956 romantic drama starring William Holden and Kim Novak. Over the course of the experiment, which was conducted every other night for six weeks, "[o]ut of the blue, it is claimed, patrons started deserting their seats and crowding around the vending machines in the lobby. Sales of Coca-Cola reportedly rose 18.1% and popcorn purchases zoomed 57.7% over the theater's usual sales."

The cause of this sudden desire for soda and popcorn?

Vicary and his "close-mouthed men" had, unbeknownst to the audiences, snuck in messages that were flashed on the screen so quickly that they could only be perceived by the subconscious—"Drink Coca-Cola" and "Eat Popcorn" (sometimes reported as "Hungry? Eat Popcorn"). Every five seconds or so, the messages would appear on the screen for a mere 1/3,000th of a second. They called it "invisible advertising," but the world would come to know it by the term Vicary coined—"subliminal advertising."

The word "subliminal" is from the Latin—*sub* or "below" and *limen* or "threshold." As the *Wall Street Journal* described it, "Patrons had been subjected to 'invisible advertising' that by-passed their conscious and assertedly struck deep into their sub-conscious."

As moviegoers at a Fort Lee theater settled in to watch Kim Novak and William Holden in the 1956 romantic drama *The Picnic*, they may have been unwitting subjects of an experiment in subliminal advertising. This lobby card was sent to such theaters to advertise the movie. *Courtesy of the Fort Lee Film Commission.*

Vicary and company had been rather secretive about the whole thing. The obvious reason was that a technology permitting advertisers to guide—or even create—consumer desires was worth a ransom. But Vicary also appreciated all those reasons the public would fear it. They decided to go public, he claimed, because "we realized what the public reaction would be, and recognized the need for public discussion. We believe its commercial use eventually may have to be under regulation of some kind, either voluntarily by the industries which use it or by the Government."

The power of the subconscious had been recognized at least as early as Sigmund Freud. Psychologists sought ways to get at that level of a person's mental processes in order to understand their choices in life. It was known that an image flashed at 1/50th of a second was fast enough for the conscious to miss but could still have an effect on the nervous system with repeated exposure. An article in the *London Sunday Times* reported on a similar experiment conducted in late 1956—interestingly enough, supposedly also in a New Jersey movie theater. The product advertised was ice cream. Dr. Arthur Koponen, a psychologist with the ad agency J. Walter Thompson, studied the idea and concluded there was plenty of experimental evidence that "perception takes place before a person is consciously aware of the stimulus." Indeed, he cited works as far back as 1863. The week prior to Vicary's press conference, Dr. Donald P. Spence and Dr. George S. Klein of New York University described experiments they performed flashing the word "angry" or "happy" over a picture of a neutral human face. Subjects described the face as either happy or sad in keeping with the word flashed over it.

But what Vicary had announced in 1957 was of greater magnitude, promising a real-world, outside-the-laboratory practical application—which is why the news spread quickly. Not only could this be applied to movies but television programs as well.

And there was something decidedly unsettling about it.

Life magazine writer Herbert Brean asked, "Could it sneak into your brain without your knowledge and make you do or feel something you did not consciously desire?'

What Vicary was describing was almost straight out of the pages of *1984*, George Orwell's seminal "Big Brother" fable. Vicary viewed it as something positive—if under proper regulation. He touted how it would offer "two substantial gains to the public: Fewer interruptions for sponsor messages and added entertainment time." He played down the notion of control, explaining that it would only serve as "reminder advertising" for products already known to the public. A subliminal ad for beer, he explained, would have no effect on a non-drinker. It would be no worse than a repetitive jingle in traditional ads.

But many others saw in it the fulfillment of their deepest fears of authoritarianism.

Vicary's announcement sent reporters scrambling to find the nearest psychologists to confirm or refute its veracity. The *Wall Street Journal*'s Carter Henderson interviewed Dr. George Klein (who had conducted the previously mentioned "angry/happy" face study the week before). He was skeptical, though perhaps it was sour grapes given how Vicary had just stolen his thunder. "Human thresholds of awareness vary greatly," he commented, "and I cannot understand how this company knows enough to subliminally project commercials effectively to a mass audience...there's no way of telling how a person will react to such an ad. He might actually form a dislike for the product."

The reaction from the advertising world was mixed. William Dye, in charge of promotions for Liebmann Breweries, Inc., would withhold judgment until he saw it himself. Stockton Helffrich from the National Broadcasting

Company (NBC) was "very interested in seeing what it's got." Harry Brandt, head of the Independent Theater Owners Association, proclaimed that he was against showing ads where people pay good money to be entertained (unlike movie theaters today!) but "wouldn't dismiss it until I had seen it."

THE HIDDEN PERSUADERS

The most explosive reaction, however, came from Vance Packard. Born in Pennsylvania in 1914, he earned his master's degree at the Columbia University Graduate School of Journalism in 1937, going on to work as a journalist with the Boston *Daily Record* before becoming an Associated Press reporter in 1940. Two years later, he moved to magazine writing and editing with publications like *American* magazine and *Collier's*. When *Collier's* went out of business, he began devoting his time completely to writing books. His best-known book was *The Hidden Persuaders,* first published in 1957. Always the social critic, Packard took on the emerging consumer culture and the techniques used to create it—including subliminal advertising. He questioned the ethics of such practices and speculated on how it might be used to subvert the democratic process. It was a bestseller, and while Packard wrote a dozen books between 1946 and 1989 (he died in 1996), it is still the one most people will have heard of.

Vicary and Packard were two ends of a controversy that had, in fact, been brewing for some time. Two years before, a BBC television station in Great Britain flashed a nonsense phrase in one of its science shows. It told the viewers something unusual had been done, but not what. They were asked to write in with what they believed it to have been. Out of 430 postcards, 20 had the phrase and 134 had at least part of it. Considering the show had 4.5 million viewers, it was a rather minor success. Similar experiments in the United States produced similarly underwhelming results.

Still, KTLA, a television station in Los Angeles, sought to be at the forefront of what it saw as the coming wave by contracting with a New Orleans company to provide subliminal ad content. The company, PRECON, was even planning a new movie release with intentional subliminal messages.

Some seemed to have a hard time taking all this psychological hocus-pocus seriously. In his 1958 *Life* magazine article, "'Hidden Sell' Technique Is Almost Here," Herbert Brean randomly sprinkled the phrase "Marilyn Monroe Call Herbert Brean" and included a stock photo at the end of the article of Marilyn making a phone call.

But not everyone found it so amusing. The National Association of Radio and Television Broadcasters—which included the three major television networks and some three hundred smaller ones—banned its members from using subliminal ads. Subliminal messaging had also caught the attention of the federal government. In January 1958, James Vicary gave a demonstration to members of an alarmed Federal Communications Commission (FCC) and Congress. The results were inconclusive. The closest thing to a success seems to have been a congressman quipping he could go for a hot dog—though the message flashed had been for popcorn. The FCC saw no need to act since there was no widespread use and the experiments were far from conclusive. Nevertheless, the New York State Senate passed legislation banning subliminal advertising, and the tide seemed definitely against the technique.

Representative William Dawson, a Republican from Utah, led a fight in Congress against subliminal ads. He wrote extensively on the matter to John C. Doerfer, the chairman of the FCC. Still, there wasn't enough evidence to support an FCC action.

The Lee

Admittedly, New Jersey is somewhat of a footnote—Vicary just happened to have supposedly selected a Fort Lee, New Jersey theater for his experiments. And yet, when this New Jersey connection is explored, the story of James Vicary's infamous experiment starts to unravel.

Nowhere in the newspaper or magazine articles that dealt with the controversy Vicary's announcement unleashed was the name of the Fort Lee theater ever given. There are possible explanations, of course. Perhaps the theater owner didn't want to be identified with such a controversial experiment. Given the claimed power of the technology and what it would be worth in dollar value, it might be in Vicary's interests to keep such details as a trade secret. After all, what if an employee at the theater told of something he saw to a competitor? That PRECON in New Orleans was signing contracts with a television station demonstrates that others would definitely want a piece of the action. Or, perhaps, the name was simply so minor a detail as to not be relevant to the greater story.

If Vicary was seeking to make it difficult to find out what theater he used for his experiment—and it's admittedly not clear he was—he could have

The Lee Theatre was the only movie house in Fort Lee at the time Vicary allegedly conducted his experiments. The marquee in this photo advertises *Stalag 17*, a Billy Wilder movie from 1953, four years before Vicary and his men arrived. *Courtesy of the Fort Lee Film Commission.*

picked a better town than Fort Lee or simply said it was "in New Jersey." According to Lucille Bertram of the Fort Lee Historical Society, "In most of 1957 there was only one operating movie theatre: the Lee Theatre. The Linwood had not yet opened and the Grant Lee was operating as a playhouse from Feb. 1957."

So anyone interested in poking around and asking questions would have little problem being sure they had the right movie theater in Fort Lee—there was only the one!

Why Vicary selected Fort Lee is unclear. Perhaps it was a name he knew from its cinematic heritage. It may have only had that single movie house in 1957, but it was once America's first "Hollywood." Cheap rent and a proximity to Manhattan helped the burgeoning cinema industries of the early twentieth century find a home in New Jersey. It also didn't hurt that Thomas Edison's Black Maria—the first American movie studio—had been located in nearby West Orange. Many of the great early movies were shot in New Jersey, particularly along the Palisades, which included Fort Lee.

Whatever the case, one man, Stuart Rogers, did indeed poke around and ask questions. In 1957, he was researching a proposed term paper on subliminal advertising as a psychology student at Hofstra College. He drove out to Fort Lee and quickly worked out it could only have been the Lee.

But it just didn't add up—literally.

Vicary claimed close to 46,000 movie patrons had been exposed to his experiment over six weeks. "The size of that small-town theater suggested it should have taken considerably longer than six weeks to complete a test of nearly 50,000 movie patrons," Rogers recalled in 1993. Perhaps most damning, however, was when he asked the theater's manager, Marvin Rosen, about it, he declared that "no such test had ever been conducted at his theater."

So was Vicary's claimed experiment a fraud? An article in *Motion Picture Daily* gave a different view. Vicary claimed that the manager never knew they conducted the experiment. It seems hard to believe no one would have noticed the subliminal projector that "was mounted on the parapet of the loge...and operated continuously...without an attendant." Further, Rosen himself was quoted as saying "several youngsters" told him that they had seen the ads.

Rosen may have known something was going on, but perhaps not what. Vicary claimed the secrecy was necessary to protect themselves for their process of filing for a patent. However, their approach to the patent seemed rather cavalier.

They had hired Floyd Crews of the New York legal firm Darby and Darby to handle the patent applications. Vicary characterized the effort as the first time one would be issued "on what is essentially a social invention." It was likened to Sigmund Freud if he had tried to get a patent on psychoanalysis. They hadn't even bothered to do the searches to see if anyone else had a patent on similar technology.

What they would have used to conduct their experiments was called a "tachistoscope." This apparatus displays an image for a specific amount of time. In and of itself, it was nothing new in 1957—the concept had been originally described by the German physiologist A.W. Volkmann in 1859, and World War II fighter pilots used them in training to quickly identify aircraft silhouettes as friends or foes. So Vicary might not have patented the equipment as much as the technique of using it. Searches of the patents and applications from the period, however, never turned up any by Vicary or his company. A version of the tachistoscope was patented, however, by his competitor, PRECON, in 1958 (issued in 1966).

The question of whether the experiment would even have been possible in the Fort Lee theater, the reported contradictory claims by the theater's manager and the lack of a patent—which was part of Vicary's explanation—have all added up to historians questioning if the experiment even took place.

In 1962, however, statements by Vicary himself would destroy his credibility.

"A Form of High Jinks"

In a September 1962 interview with Fred Danzig for *Advertising Age* magazine, Vicary recalled viewing subliminal advertising at first as "a form of high jinks I didn't want to have anything to do with." Nevertheless, he came around to investigating the possibilities with the idea of applying for a patent should it pan out. The experiments at Fort Lee were the beginnings of that process. Things became complicated, however, by what he claimed was a leak of information that jeopardized the whole plan. With only the single experiment under their belt, he felt their hand had been forced and he had to come forward with his press release to stake his claim of priority.

Vicary maintained that they had done the experiment but that they were forced into a premature announcement of their findings. "Worse than the timing, though, was the fact that we hadn't done any research, except what was needed for filing a patent," he said. "I had only...a small amount of data—too small to be meaningful. And what we had shouldn't have been used promotionally."

The nuance of the answer is important. In the decades since, Vicary has been portrayed as a fraud, suspected of making up his Fort Lee data and even accused of having never really carried out the experiment at all. Indeed, many cite this 1962 interview as his admission of falsifying his Fort Lee test.

And yet, that really isn't what he said.

He would maintain until his death in 1977 that the Fort Lee experiment was real—only that the results were released prematurely and should not have been announced so soon without further corroborative tests. It is possible to interpret from his statements that he perhaps exaggerated the numbers to bolster support. But he seems to have taken a gamble that further testing would verify what he felt he had been forced to prematurely announce. If so, it was a gamble he lost. In the end, he didn't view subliminal advertising as a hoax but, rather, was forced to conclude it had been "a gimmick" that failed.

Kelly B. Crandall, who researched the Vicary controversy, concluded, "When the Danzig interview is situated with earlier evidence, it provides a realistic possibility that an experiment of some kind took place, but that Vicary exaggerated the ensuing results for the sake of publicity."

Whatever the truth, James Vicary retreated from the public spotlight. It is not clear if he ever made an application for a patent, but one was never granted—a fact some cite as proof of his fraud. He has grown into something of a shady, Svengali-type figure in the history of pop culture and advertising. Rumors spread that he had become very wealthy off his ill-gotten gains and retreated from the public eye to a life of luxury. After all, a 1957 *Newsweek* article stated that Vicary had spoken to 250 companies about subliminal advertising contracts. But even this would appear to have been an effort to spin him into a villain. Speaking with companies is different than actually signing contracts, and even if he had done some consulting work for any of them, the numbers thrown around seem to have been gross exaggerations of the fees typical of the period.

In any event, Vicary's reputation was ruined by the whole affair. He did indeed leave the country but claimed it was to escape the scandal, heading on a whim to England to see the birthplace of his father. Upon his return, he had an unlisted phone number out of fear for his life caused by hostile letters to the editors of publications covering the controversy.

SEX IN AN ICE CUBE

Does subliminal advertising work? Some experiments seem to indicate it can, though not so well as to be really useful, and that it is dependent on a wide range of factors. Periodically, researchers seem to rediscover the idea, and conspiracy theorists always see it as a sinister plot by someone.

In 1973, Wilson B. Key's book *Subliminal Seduction* picked up where Vance Packard had left off, claiming to see secret symbols and words in print ads—including the word "sex" in the ice cubes pictured in a liquor ad. It raised new concerns over the practice, and the FCC finally passed a ban on it in January 1974, stating that whether or not it was effective, it was contrary to the public well-being.

We still live in Vicary's shadow—in 1978, the police in Wichita, Kansas, asked KAKE-TV to insert subliminal messages in its news reports about the "BTK Killer" (Bind, Torture, Kill) to convince him to turn himself in (it didn't work); French president François Mitterrand had subliminal images of himself mixed in the title sequence of a French national news show during the 1988 election; in 2000, a TV ad campaign ran by Republicans for George W. Bush included the word "BUREAUCRATS" but then one frame showing only "RATS" over Al Gore's image (the FCC investigated but no actions were taken); the British alternative comedy show *The Young Ones* included obvious subliminal images as a goof on the concept; the horror film *The Exorcist* included many subliminal images said to increase the movie's effect; the McDonald's logo appeared in a single frame of the Food Network's hit show *Iron Chef* in 2007, though they claimed it was an unintentional glitch.

Whether done seriously or in jest, subliminal messages have a certain dark lure—one that destroyed James Vicary. The controversy rears its head every so often and, for better or worse, will likely do so into the future with each new wave of technology in our mass media culture.

And, to a large degree, we can trace it all to a darkened theater in Fort Lee, New Jersey.

Garden State Legacy #3, March 2008

CHAPTER 3

Train Talk

How New Jersey's Belvidere–Delaware Branch of the
PRR Helped Modernize Rail Communication

How many ways can you think of to communicate with someone who is not nearby? You can call them on the ubiquitous cell phone that seems to hang from everyone's belt. You could text-message them on a Blackberry or iPhone. You could send an email or post a "tweet" on Twitter or a "status update" on Facebook, communicating with large numbers of people all at once. You could radio them or send a fax. In short, there is a generation of Americans who will grow up having never known what it's like to *not* be connected by technology to the greater world. But there was a time, not all that long ago, when it wasn't so easy—no phones, no radio and certainly no Internet.

Now imagine you're the engineer of a steam locomotive. How would you communicate with the brakeman in the caboose or with the stationmaster at the next station? If you could see each other, you could use hand signals, flags or lamps—all of which were used by railroaders of old. Indeed, they still do today. Watch the conductors on a passenger train when they're on the platform during a station stop. Once everyone is onboard, they will use hand or flashlight signals to let the engineer know that it's safe to start moving again.

Perhaps the most charming mode of communication, however, is also that most quintessential sound of the rails—the train whistle. By combining long and short blasts from whistles on the engine and caboose, one end of the train could "talk" to the other, even when out of direct sight, as on a curve or at night. It's also a good way to get the attention of anyone along the way. One long blast still warns people on the station platform that the train is

In the era before radio, communicating with a moving train was accomplished using the limited vocabulary of whistles. *Courtesy of the author.*

approaching. Most people today will recognize the two long, one short and one long as the warning that a train is approaching a road crossing.

Knowing how to "speak" in whistle blasts and visual signals were skills every train crew needed to master, and they served the industry well into the early twentieth century. Nevertheless, it was a limited vocabulary. If a train stopped unexpectedly, the brakeman in the service car (also known as the "caboose" or "crummy") would need to walk all the way to the engine to find out what the trouble was—and some freight trains could be miles long!

Clearly, as radio and telephone technology matured at the last turn of the century, there would be attempts at implementing them on the rails. Yet, they presented some serious technical and, surprisingly, even political challenges that would need to be overcome first.

PHONES AND RADIOS

Before the era of the cell phone, telephone communications relied on both parties being connected by lengths of wire—often thousands of miles worth—to carry the signal. Telephone lines could certainly be strung from one end of a train to the other. Indeed, by the early 1940s, luxury passenger trains built by the Pullman company had boasted telephone communications. But these were "fixed-consist" trains, meaning that once the cars were strung together, they stayed that way for the duration of the trip.

Freight trains were a different matter. Even if the more than two million freight cars throughout the United States in the first half of the twentieth century could have been wired economically, the system only worked when the cars were coupled together so that the telephone lines could be connected. As a matter of course with freights, the "consist"—the makeup of the cars—changes as parts of the train are dropped off along the way or other cars picked up. The phone line connections would be broken during these decoupling and coupling maneuvers, making it useless. If cars became decoupled by an accident while the train was running, the phone communications would be down at the very time they could be most important! Indeed, as we shall see, it was this very situation that had jump-started research into rail communications. Further, such an arrangement would not allow the moving train to communicate with stations and the block controllers along the way.

The emerging technology of radio held more promise. It was already being used for aviation—for aircraft-to-aircraft and aircraft-to-ground communications. It was tougher, however, for the railroads to utilize this technology. As the commercial radio industry grew in the early twentieth century, there was much competition for the available wave bands. It was difficult for the FCC authorities responsible for licensing and assigning frequencies to give suitable bands to the numerous railroads throughout the nation.

Further, radio waves are difficult to keep confined within the relatively short distances and narrow space from one end of a train to another or even within the bounds of a typical rail yard. There was an obvious issue with interference from other sources along the way. These were also the days before FM radio, so signals could fade out when the train passed under a bridge or was inside a tunnel. There were some experiments being conducted, but FM was not yet in widespread use by the Second World War. The war itself had diverted many research resources from the private sector to the more pressing military needs.

According to an article appearing in the October 1944 issue of *Railroad Magazine*, "Train Talk. Carrier System for End-to-End Communication Speeds Up Freights on Pennsy Branch Line," M.S. Newman described how "a number of the larger lines, Baltimore and Ohio, Burlington, D&RGW,

Rock Island, and Santa Fe are conducting experiments with 'walkie-talkie' outfits, ultra-high-frequency sets, and the applications of the newly-developed frequency-modulation techniques." He noted, "When wide-scale trials have been made, there's bound to be something new to add to the history of radio in train communication."

WRECK

While Newman doesn't mention it, the fact that his article was appearing at the time it did hints at the broader political back story involved. The Pennsylvania Railroad had been under fire as a result of a deadly wreck in North Carolina that had occurred almost a year earlier, in December 1943.

According to an article by James Alexander Jr. in the May 1995 issue of *Milepost*, the journal of the Friends of the Railroad Museum of Pennsylvania, "A broken rail had derailed the last three cars of the West Coast Champion, traveling southbound at 85 mph. Separated from the rest of the train, the derailed cars remained upright, fouling the northbound track, while the rest of the consist—three diesels and fifteen passenger cars—came to an emergency stop half a mile beyond. While passengers were being evacuated from the derailed cars (there were no serious injuries), a brakeman was sent to halt any following traffic."

Whenever a train came to an unexpected stop, the brakeman, fireman or conductor would walk down the tracks from the rear of the train with flags, lanterns or flares in order to warn trains coming up from behind to stop.

The conductor up near the engine, however, wasn't aware of the decoupled cars. All he found was minor damage to the coupling and air line between two cars near the front and assumed this was the reason they had stopped. He was unable to see that three of his cars were missing off the back end thanks to the dark of night and a blinding snowstorm. "Lantern signals from the rear were obscured and misinterpreted," explains Alexander. The engineer sent his fireman (formerly the crew member who fed the coal into the furnace of the steam locomotives and, here, an assistant to the engineer in a diesel) to also help warn the train due behind them. As Alexander described it, "The fireman too was unaware of the derailed cars behind his train. He carried lanterns and one fusee [a type of flare], but in the excitement he neglected to take additional fusees...[s]ighting the headlight of the northbound train, the fireman attempted to light his only fusee, slipped on the icy ballast, and broke it. His efforts to flag down the fast-approaching express hurtling along at 85 mph with his flickering lanterns were to no avail...Roaring on by the halted southbound, the northbound slammed into the protruding derailed passenger cars, and the ensuing calamity became the next day's headlines."

Seventy people lost their lives in the wreck, including forty-seven U.S. servicemen. The subsequent investigations blamed human error. Nevertheless, *New York Times* columnist and radio commentator Drew Pearson assumed that a new technology being developed, the radio-telephone, would have allowed the crews to communicate and avoid the tragedy. Why, he asked, hadn't the Pennsylvania Railroad—one of the most powerful railroads in the Northeast—been making use of this technology? Their neglect of such advances, he asserted, as good as cost those people their lives. Rail historians, however, tend to discount that it would have made a difference, since each of the crews never knew the full extent of the damage to the train.

But once Pearson raged against the Pennsylvania Railroad for being so technologically backward, the thing took on a life of its own. Letters to the editor started appearing, and politicians could smell a good cause to adopt.

Under pressure from the Interstate Commerce Commission (ICC), the FCC got into the act, working with the ICC to push radio use on the rails. According to Alexander, "Public pressure was still on. *Railway Age* [January 6, 1945] noted that 'after being practically dormant since 1930, intense interest in train communication burst forth in February, 1944, and has continued at white heat since that time.'"

Journalist Drew Pearson later in his career with President Lyndon Johnson. In 1943, it was his criticism of the Pennsylvania Railroad following a tragic wreck that pressured a renewed effort to improve rail communications.

The irony is that part of the PRR's backwardness had been imposed by the very government that was then forcing the issue. With a war on, research resources were being channeled into the effort. Radios were needed by the military, and few were available for such civilian experimentations.

The human cost aside, the PRR was facing a public relations nightmare. Fair or not, it was being criticized on a systemic level for an accident that killed not only civilians, but also servicemen during wartime—servicemen who were on leave just before Christmas, no less.

It was no coincidence then that Newman's piece in *Railroad Magazine* appeared when it did in October 1944. It was, in effect, part of an overall campaign by the PRR and its federal overseers—the railroads were being run by the U.S. Army—for damage control.

It could be argued, however, that regardless of the inspiration, it provided a needed catalyst in rail communication development. All they needed was a good rail line on which to test all this new technology.

And they found it in New Jersey.

BEL-DEL

When we want to take a train somewhere inside New Jersey these days, we really only have one choice—New Jersey Transit. Heading outside the Garden State, of course, we have Amtrak and the links of PATH into Manhattan and SEPTA to Philadelphia. But taking the train in this state is a fairly straightforward thing. Even freight lines are limited to a handful, such as Norfolk Southern and CSX. This state of affairs belies the more complex beginnings of railroading around here and in the nation.

In the early days, rail lines were established between specific local points in order to serve specific local needs. On February 6, 1815, the New Jersey Railroad Company became the first such enterprise chartered in the United States with the intention of linking New Brunswick with Trenton. While it never got as far as actually laying tracks, it did at least provide the model for future railroads. On February 3, 1840, the first U.S. railroad, the Camden and Amboy (C&A) Rail Road and Transportation Company, was chartered, linking Camden, New Jersey, and Perth Amboy. Bridges and ferries extended links into New York City and Philadelphia. The C&A had imported the first practical steam locomotive from England for use on its line. Known as the John Bull, it still survives at the Smithsonian Institution and was actually restored to running condition in 1981.

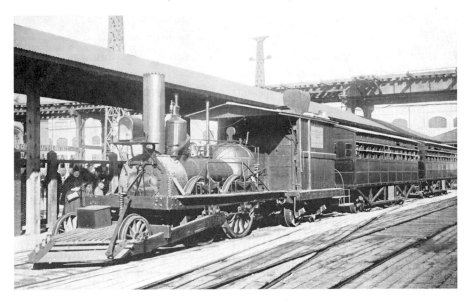

The first practical steam locomotive, known as the John Bull, ran on New Jersey's Camden and Amboy Rail Road. It is seen here on display at the World Columbian Exposition in Chicago in 1893.

As New Jersey's population increased, spotting the map with more towns and factories, additional short lines were established and merged into expanding regional railroads. Rails both traced and drove the development of the state's industries and communities to a degree not seen again until the introduction of the automobile. This gave the railroads inordinate influence over the state and local governments—New Jersey became known derisively as "The State of Camden and Amboy" at the height of the C&A's powers.

A good example, however, of how local short lines evolved into regional systems can be found in the Belvidere and Delaware Railroad. Chartered March 2, 1836, it sought to link Trenton with Belvidere along the Delaware River but also to connect with a planned railroad that would run west to the Susquehanna River in Pennsylvania.

The company would pretty much exist only on paper at first, though the idea was still considered sound enough that the Camden and Amboy Rail Road bought stock in what was nicknamed the "Bel-Del" on February 29, 1838. But it wasn't until February 6, 1851—fifteen years after its charter—that the first rails were opened from Trenton north to Lambertville. A station was built at Trenton on April 25 at Warren Street. The line would be extended four times until finally linking with its namesake terminus of Belvidere on November 5, 1855.

Once established, the line was branched out over the years in various ways. In 1854, for example, Bel-Del agreed to operate the Flemington Railroad and Transportation Company, which added a branch from Lambertville northeast to Flemington. The Lehigh Valley Railroad coal trains started using the Bel-Del on January 17, 1856, linking with it at Phillipsburg. That summer, a stagecoach route was initiated linking the town of Belvidere with the Delaware, Lackawanna and Western (DL&W) Railroad at Delaware, New Jersey. This provided connection for passengers continuing west into Pennsylvania, but it was replaced on May 16, 1864, by an extension of the Bel-Del rails to the DL&W at Manunka Chunk. This made life a little easier for commuters, though they would still need to transfer trains. The gauge of the tracks—the space between rails and, therefore, between the wheels of the train—had not been standardized, and the two railroads ran different gauges. Once they became standardized, through service was finally offered in 1876.

Passenger service was extended into Philadelphia in 1865 when it linked to the Philadelphia and Trenton Railroad. Connecting with Philadelphia was important for another reason. On April 1, 1872, the juggernaut Pennsylvania Railroad began operating the Bel-Del under the new name of the Belvidere Division of the United Railroads of New Jersey, Grand Division.

And still, the Bel-Del grew. It merged with the Flemington Railroad and Transportation Company on February 16, 1885, forming the Belvidere and Delaware Railroad. On April 14, 1896, the Enterprise Railroad and Martins Creek Railroad were merged into the Bel-Del. The Lehigh and Hudson River Railway acquired trackage rights (the rights to run its trains on the Bel-Del tracks) on its line from Belvidere south to Phillipsburg in 1889. In 1908, the Pennsylvania Railroad added trackage rights over the Delaware, Lackawanna and Western Railroad from Manunka Chunk northwest to East Stroudsburg for trains serving the Pocono resorts.

It was on this matured Bel-Del branch that the Pennsylvania Railroad would test its technology—and attempt to deflect some of the criticism over the North Carolina tragedy.

RADIO-PHONE

Author M.S. Newman described the Bel-Del as particularly ideal for the test. "With limited passenger service, and ten or twelve freights on schedule daily," he wrote, "this single-track branch...supplies service for local industries en route, connecting at Phillipsburg, N.J., with heavy-duty shipments from the large cement-manufacturing plants around Easton, Pa., just across the [Delaware] river...'Nothin' better'n the Bel-Del,' old heads will tell you when you go down to take a look at operations. Most of the railroaders there are veterans of this road up to the beautiful Delaware Water Gap country, and have put in a good part of their years of service there. And now that the Bel-Del boasts the most extensive train communication system in regular use on any line today, you'll have to admit that the old heads have a real point in their favor."

As an example of how it all worked, Newman looked at Engine No. 3784, a Class L-1 Mikado type, which was hauling a string of boxcars. "Inside the cab," he wrote, "placed conveniently for the engineer, is a microphone of the kind used on ordinary telephones, mounted in a handset of the French type, with an ear-phone at the other end. It hangs from a hook at the side of

The tubes of the radio-phone system were protected by rubber in a box mounted on the locomotive's running board. Such a box can be seen in this photo of a Mikado-class steam locomotive. *Courtesy of Mike Carter.*

small square control box, which contains the mechanism for controlling the volume of the voice current. A loudspeaker is suspended from the cab roof... [t]ransmitter and receiver, with the necessary tubes, filters, etc., are mounted in rubber and set in an oblong, all-steel box, which is placed on the running board."

A similar setup would be in the caboose. This system transmitted the signal by using the rails as the wires. "[The r]eceiving apparatus consists of coils mounted underneath the body of the vehicle, which pick up the current in the track by induction."

During the example trip, the train came to an unexpected stop. The engineer, H.A. Scholl—"a tall, sparse veteran of the Bel-Del"—called from the locomotive's cab to conductor J.J. Schumacher in the service car. There were nineteen freight cars between them, but the engineer was able to let his conductor know "[t]here's an automobile stalled on the grade crossing up ahead, and they're just getting it moved out of the way. We'll have about a five minutes' wait, I think."

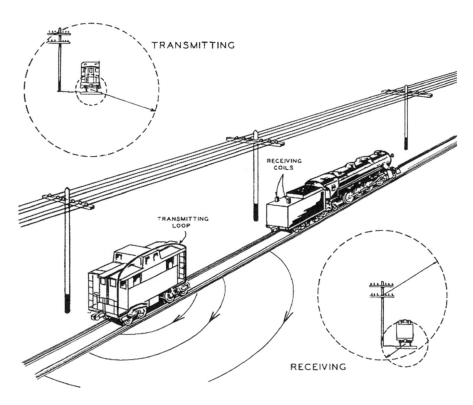

This diagram, showing how the radio-phone induction system worked, accompanied M.S. Newman's *Railroad Magazine* 1944 article. *Courtesy of the author.*

"Saves me a trip," conductor Schumacher commented to the brakeman, V.M. Satterfield. "Used to be I'd have to walk up to the head end and find out what's going on. Nineteen cars isn't so far, but often we have three or four times this many, more than half a mile."

Telephone wires alongside the tracks allowed the train crews to also communicate with stations and the block operators responsible for clearing trains to enter or leave their section of track, or block. Previously, new orders for the train crews would need to be retrieved by hand—no small task when the train is moving! The written orders would be handed off using a stick shaped like a Y with string across the open forks at the top. The written orders would be tied to the string, and someone would have to stand at the side of the track, holding the frame aloft. The engineer or conductor would snatch the stick out of his hand by getting an arm through the forks and under the string. If he missed, the train would need to be stopped and the orders delivered by hand, wasting valuable time. Imagine doing this in the dark or during a storm or in fog! With the new technology, however, the engineer could speak directly to the station or block operator.

Another application was assisting with the various tests performed on each train before it was allowed to leave the yard. And, if a malfunction occurred in the middle between the engine and caboose, where the train crews might not see it, an observer at a station could then easily report it to the crew after they passed.

Proving the system could be of value in a crisis was of obvious importance, and Newman was able to cite an example of just that. A freight heading south between Trenton and Phillipsburg came to an abrupt stop. There was smoke rising from a little bridge up ahead. The engineer was able to report it to the block operator in Frenchtown, who sent a nearby work train that had firefighting equipment. Another freight that had been in a siding also heard the report and was warned about the problem before proceeding. Thanks to the quick communications, the fire was put out before it could do any serious damage. "By means of train communication," Newman crowed, "between moving units and way stations, a minor emergency was handled in double-quick time before it had any chance of tying up the line."

Clearly the New Jersey experiment was the proof of concept—and proof of action in response to a problem—that the PRR needed. It's likely that Newman's article was due in part to the media blitz undertaken in February 1944 by the railroad's general superintendent of telegraph, W.R. Triem. Press releases were issued, and he even went on a speaking tour. In an effort to allay the fears of the traveling public and quiet critics, he called the successful Bel-Del tests the "latest of a long list of improvements developed by the PRR and other railroads in cooperation with various electrical manufacturers to expedite train movements and afford better service to the public."

The Association of American Railroads (AAR) had supported the PRR's actions and defended it against its critics. It had been the AAR that approached Washington about conducting tests and that had pointed out the difficulties the wartime restrictions had created. Together, the AAR and PRR had kept a close watch on Drew Pearson's commentaries, trying to set him straight on the facts of the accident that had so unleashed his wrath.

But now they could back it up with concrete improvements. It was announced that the Pennsylvania Railroad would install this new "Trainphone" on the 245-mile, four-track route between Harrisburg and Pittsburgh. Once World War II ended, the civilian world reaped the benefits of a host of technologies developed mostly in secret by the government—radar, sonar, microwaves and more portable communications. This helped the rail communications as well. By 1950, 1,613 miles of track on the PRR had Trainphone service. Managers of other branches visited the Bel-Del to see the equipment in action and soon were ordering it for their lines as well.

An illustration of an engineman using the radio-phone in the cab. *Courtesy of the author.*

TRANSITIONS

Ironically, though the PRR could tout itself as being ahead of the curve when it came to this induction carrier system in the 1940s, it was its adherence to it—perhaps due to having invested much in its development—that put it behind again in the 1950s.

"As a result of its public hearings, in May 1945," Alexander comments, "the FCC assigned 60 clear channels for railroad use, each channel 60 kilohertz wide, between 152 and 162 megahertz. (The number of channels and their width subsequently changed as a result of technological refinements and other needs.)"

Not all railroads had adopted the induction method, and once the FCC started freeing up frequencies, they were quick to hop on the radio bandwagon.

According to Alexander, "In the early 1950s, American railroads were installing over 2,300 radios a year, but the Pennsy installed only limited radio yard communications (such as at its Sunnyside yard) later in the decade. For some years the PRR continued to show its Trainphones in advertising, and it did serve a major purpose. By 1952, it had installed 1,268 Trainphones."

By the early 1960s, the PRR management was facing the reality that while its Trainphone induction-based system had worked well, it was fast becoming obsolete. Since it was the only major buyer for the equipment, no manufacturers had bothered to try to update it. Installation and maintenance would be cheaper for a new radio system than the existing Trainphone. Another major factor was that the induction system couldn't work on electrified rails. In short, the technology that had pushed it to the fore was now a dead end.

The transition to transistors began in 1966. With its General Order No. 2220, effective April 30, 1967, the PRR officially stopped using the induction system in favor of the radios. As Alexander put it, "Thus a useful but now outdated example of railroading progress came to an abrupt end."

These days, advances such as computers and satellite monitoring of trains help the railroads operate in ways the "old heads" could never have imagined. Such technologies have even made the caboose—and the very need for the end-to-end communication—a thing of the past.

The Bel-Del itself has also gone through changes. Mother Nature dealt it a blow in August 1955, when Hurricane Diane washed out the tracks north of Belvidere. In what was the beginning of the end, that stretch of tracks was abandoned, and at the end of 1957, the Bel-Del was absorbed into the

United New Jersey Railroad and Canal Company, though the Pennsylvania Railroad remained the parent company.

The real end came in April 1976 when the once-mighty PRR went bankrupt and was turned into the federally funded Conrail. The line from Milford south to Trenton was converted into part of the Delaware and Raritan Canal State Park.

Large portions of Conrail were taken over by Norfolk Southern in the 1990s and now operate the line north to Belvidere. In 1995, the tracks from Milford north to Phillipsburg were taken over by the Belvidere and Delaware River Railway—a short line railroad company like back in the old days.

The story of this interesting bit of New Jersey's railroad history has come full circle.

Garden State Legacy #4, June 2008

CHAPTER 4

Scooping Sputnik 2

How America Learned of Sputnik 2 from New Jersey

I t was shortly before 1:00 a.m. when the voice crackled out of the static. "Stand by for a special bulletin," it commanded in Russian.

George Chaplenko, a thirty-three-year-old man living in Perth Amboy, listened closely. He could easily understand what the announcer on his short-wave radio was saying—not only because he had recently emigrated from the Ukraine but also because he had been conscripted into the Russian army during the Second World War.

As he listened to the broadcast from Moscow coming through the darkness, perhaps he had a flicker of a memory from those days in the war and of being captured by the Germans and sent to the forced labor camp. He needed only to have glanced at the identification numbers tattooed on his wrist to be reminded.

But he also needed only to look at his wife, Tatiana.

They had met at the camp, and their wedding picture was taken on a U.S. Army jeep when the Americans liberated them. An army chaplain did the honors.

Chaplenko and his bride came to the United States in 1949 as refugees. A bright young man, Chaplenko found work as a chemist and engineer with the Singer Sewing Machine Company.

His work hours brought him home at 11:00 p.m.—just when the long-distance frequencies he was interested in came in clearest due to atmospheric ionization conditions. So, in the small hours of November 3, 1957, he was focused on that voice coming from his short-wave radio. He had only recently started listening in, inspired by the article "Listen to the Voices of

George Chaplenko. *Courtesy of Amateur Astronomers, Inc.*

the World" in that month's *Popular Electronics* that had provided the program schedule for the twenty-meter band broadcasted from Moscow.

Figuring this special news bulletin had to be something important, he switched on his tape recorder, and what he heard shocked him: "We have just launched a second Earth satellite."

Not only had the Russians once again beaten the United States in the nascent "space race," but this time they upped the stakes by sending a living being—a dog—into orbit.

This was big—the proverbial "Stop the presses!" kind of big.

Excitedly, Chaplenko started calling the newspapers, including the *New York Times*. Reporters receiving the calls at one o'clock in the morning from an excited man with a foreign accent about the Reds sending a dog into space were not amused. He was dismissed as a crank and told to turn off his radio and go back to bed. Still, he insisted on leaving his name and telephone number.

Hours later, word was coming from London that they were picking up an English-language version of the same announcement. Suddenly George Chaplenko's phone didn't stop ringing.

Space Race

It is perhaps difficult for us today to appreciate what a shock this news was to the American psyche. We had been feeling pretty good about ourselves after our role in winning World War II. We had emerged on the world stage as a true global power. Thanks to two oceans and friendly neighbors, the industrial might that powered our war effort was left unmolested. The huge demand for consumer goods by a society weary of the Great Depression and austerity measures of wartime launched a period of economic prosperity not since paralleled. The only clouds on our bright, shiny horizon were the Soviet Union and Communist China, each of which presented competition for the spoils of Europe and Asia, respectively. But certainly, we assured ourselves, the nation that had just won a world war and invented frozen TV dinners could take on all comers!

The terrible power of the atomic bombs dropped on Japan was still fresh in our collective memories. And these city-obliterating bombs were mere firecrackers compared with the increasingly powerful bombs being developed at the time. There was a marriage going on of this technology with the rockets the Nazis had used toward the end of the war to worry London. It was only a matter of time before the orders of magnitude grew great enough that missiles, topped with nuclear warheads, could deliver their awful packages across the globe to American cities.

The United States was shocked, not only that the Russians had beat them into space again but that this time included a living passenger as well. *Courtesy of the* Times *of Trenton.*

Viewed in terms of a war for the ideological dominance of the world, the very thought that the Soviets could launch payloads into orbit led directly to a scary conclusion. At first, it was just a basketball-sized beeping sphere, but now it was a capsule with a living creature. Tomorrow it might be a nuclear bomb. And, if they could achieve a permanent orbit, so the logic went, they could hold the entire United States hostage with the threat of lobbing warheads on us at will from outer space—and there was nothing we could do about it.

Sputnik 2 was a large spacecraft. Where Sputnik 1 weighed only 167 pounds, this one weighed in at 1,120 pounds—about as large as a one-hundred-kiloton nuclear warhead. Furthermore, both Sputniks 1 and 2 had a third stage to their rocket capable of lifting ten tons into low orbit—the size of a half-megaton bomb. It meant the Russians were at least capable of lobbing those kinds of weapons.

There are technical reasons why this probably could never have really happened. But this vision of an atomic age Sword of Damocles was what would drive much of the thinking behind the American space program for a generation.

The news that crackled out of George Chaplenko's radio in those early morning hours was more than just a stunt. It was Russian one-upmanship in what was seen as a deadly serious competition.

LAIKA

Sputnik 2 was the second in a series of spacecraft that would be launched by the Soviet Union between 1957 and 1961, initiated by the International Geophysical Year. The full name *Prosteyshiy Sputnik 2* translated into "elementary traveler," or in this context, a "satellite" to Earth. It would be applied to a wide range of robotic craft, ranging from the simple beeping sphere of Sputnik 1 to test craft for manned flight to probes to the moon, Venus and Mars.

What made this second launch different from anything attempted before by either the USSR or the United States was that Sputnik 2 carried a live passenger, a dog named Laika. She was a three-year-old mongrel found wandering the streets of Moscow—the scientists figured such a stray would already be tough from life on the mean streets in the cold and heat. Her story, however, is a sad one. No attempts would be made to recover the spacecraft, dooming her to also become the first casualty in space. The "training" she endured was harsh, keeping her in progressively smaller cages to get her used to being in a tiny capsule. One of the trainers brought her home to play with his children as a last gesture of kindness before sending her on her one-way voyage.

The plan was that Laika would be euthanized with a poisoned serving of food after ten days. In 2002, however, Dr. Dimitri Malashenkov confirmed what some had heard rumored. The thermal insulation ripped off after launch, and Laika died of stress and overheating only hours later.

There had always been something unsettling about Laika's fate. Organizations against cruelty to animals throughout the world roundly criticized the Soviets for it. In 1998, after the fall of the Soviet Union, Oleg Gazenko, one of the scientists responsible for sending Laika into space, expressed regrets even all those years later. What little they actually learned about the ability of higher organisms to live in space simply did not justify the death of Laika.

It is worth noting that in the four subsequent Sputnik missions involving dogs, retrieval would be incorporated (though one mission failed, resulting in the deaths of the two dogs onboard). The United States used monkeys and chimpanzees with varying degrees of success.

The ethics of using animals in a range of testing are still hotly debated.

Laika's fate angered animal rights activists, and animal testing remains a controversial issue. *Courtesy of Tass/Sovfoto.*

GEORGE

Once the truth of the launch had been confirmed, the rush was on in the media to get the scoop—and for a while, the only U.S. source for information was that chemist with the funny accent from Perth Amboy whom they had initially dismissed as a crank!

The *New York Times* ran a piece titled "Jerseyan First to Report News; Perth Amboy Chemist Hears Broadcast from Moscow Announcing Launch." The entire article cites George Chaplenko as the sole source.

"The first report of the launching of a new Soviet satellite came this morning from a New Jersey chemist...This transmission preceded the English broadcast that was picked up in London," the *Times* reported. "Mr. Chaplenko, who was born in the Ukraine and came to this country as a refugee, immediately called the *New York Times*. He reported that he first heard the announcement at 12:45 A.M. It was repeated several times, he said." At first, it wasn't clear what time the satellite had actually been launched. Chaplenko inferred from the broadcast that it had to have been the previous day, Saturday, November 2, 1957.

Wondering what else the Russians might have in store and sensing the opportunity for a scoop, the *New York Times* gave George Chaplenko the assignment of listening in on subsequent short-wave broadcasts for more news. While there was no new space news, he did record and transcribe the entire speech of Nikita Khruschev on the anniversary of the Russian Revolution. Thanks to George, the *Times* foreign-news editor had the text hours before the normal channels of translation via London. "I might make this short-wave listening a business instead of a hobby if my luck continues," Chaplenko quipped to *Popular Electronics* magazine, which issued a press release in honor of the coup scored by one of its readers.

Indeed, the magazine reaped a windfall of sales—the issue Chaplenko had used to find the correct wavelengths was selling off the newsstand shelves. For his efforts on its behalf, the *New York Times* paid him twenty-five dollars.

Chaplenko would go on to earn a bachelor's degree in mechanical engineering and a master's degree in spectroscopy. He put the latter to good use at what was then called SPEX Industries in Metuchen, New Jersey, where he made spectrometers. Over the years, he would even have numerous patents to his name—the last awarded in 2000 for an improved industrial grinding mill. But perhaps most telling of his intellectual prowess is a story his old friends still fondly tell of how, long after he had retired,

The New York Times

TIMES SQUARE NEW YORK 36 N Y
LAckawanna 4-1000

Nov. 4, 1957

Mr. George Chaplemko,
276 Goodwin Street,
Perth Amboy, N.J.

Dear Mr. Chaplemko:

Thank you very much for your help on
the satellite story on Sunday morning. I
am enclosing a copy of the story we ran in
our late editions, in case you missed it.
I am also authorizing a payment of $25.00
for your expenses and help. This should arrive
in a week or so.

Sincerely,

Harold Faber
Day National News
Editor

LT
Encl.

Right: The letter George Chaplenko received from the *New York Times*, thanking him for his "scoop" on the Sputnik 2 story. *Courtesy of Alan and Bonnie Witzgall, Amateur Astronomers, Inc.*

Below: Chaplenko received twenty-five dollars for his story. *Courtesy of Alan and Bonnie Witzgall, Amateur Astronomers, Inc.*

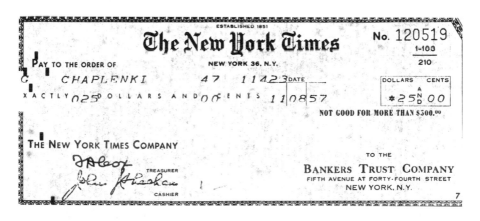

The New York Times

ESTABLISHED 1851

No. 120519
1-100

NEW YORK 36, N.Y.
210

PAY TO THE ORDER OF

G CHAPLENKI   47   1142 3 DATE

DOLLARS   CENTS

EXACTLY 025 DOLLARS AND 00 CENTS 11 08 57

*25 00

NOT GOOD FOR MORE THAN $500.00

THE NEW YORK TIMES COMPANY

TREASURER

CASHIER

TO THE

BANKERS TRUST COMPANY
FIFTH AVENUE AT FORTY-FOURTH STREET
NEW YORK, N.Y.

Singer would still call on him as a consultant to solve particularly tough engineering problems that had stumped younger men.

He indulged a lifelong passion for amateur astronomy by making homemade telescopes and joining Amateur Astronomers, Inc., a club based in Cranford, New Jersey, in 1972. He served as AAI's vice-president

(1974–1977) and president (1977–1980) and is still warmly remembered as someone who encouraged young people to join and become active— sometimes to the annoyance of the older, more staid members. These days, many of those young people—who refer to themselves as having been the "young Jedi knights"—are now the elder statesmen of the club and carry on the tradition of making sure young people are welcomed and encouraged.

He served as the group's corresponding secretary from 1984 until his death on November 16, 2004.

George could often be found standing outside AAI's Sperry Observatory, in his loud checked jacket and baseball hat, a cigarette always in his hand and ready with a smile or a corny joke. His warmth and generosity are still remembered. It remains a source of pride that the Western Hemisphere first heard the news of Sputnik 2 thanks to this Ukrainian refugee from Perth Amboy and his late-night short-wave radio hobby.

Garden State Legacy #4, June 2008

CHAPTER 5

The Constitutional Courant

Was New Jersey's First Printer Responsible for New York's Most Virulent Anti–Stamp Act Broadsides?

S ince the last which I had the honour to write to you of the 23d of September this town has remained quiet," New York's lieutenant governor, Cadwallader Colden, wrote to the British secretary of state for America, Henry Seymour Conway, on November 12, 1765.

For Colden, it was a welcomed respite from what had been a politically embarrassing time. The Stamp Act of 1765 has gone down in history as among the seminal Parliamentary policies responsible for driving the wedge between Great Britain and the North American colonies. The act called for a direct tax on paper, requiring all printed matter produced in the colonies to be on "stamped" paper to show that the tax had indeed been paid. And that covered a lengthy list of things, indeed—everything from newspapers to playing cards.

Such taxes were nothing new. Indeed, New York and Massachusetts had both imposed stamp taxes in the previous decade, though they were repealed after failing to raise enough revenue. People back in England were long used to such measures. Since pretty much everyone used some form of product involving paper, there was a presumed equity in such a tax. Certainly some businesses required more paper than others, but it didn't single out any specific group of users.

So there was no reason for Parliament to think it would be such a big deal in 1765. Besides, the Crown had just assumed a big debt to pay for all those troops that had recently won the Seven Years' War against France—effectively securing North America for British interests. Since the French had been threatening the colonists' collective backyard for years,

(279)

Anno quinto

Georgii III. Regis.

C A P. XII.

An Act for granting and applying certain Stamp Duties, and other Duties, in the *British* Colonies and Plantations in *America*, towards further defraying the Expences of defending, protecting, and securing the same; and for amending such Parts of the several Acts of Parliament relating to the Trade and Revenues of the said Colonies and Plantations, as direct the Manner of determining and recovering the Penalties and Forfeitures therein mentioned.

WHEREAS by an Act made in the last Session of Parliament, several Duties were granted, continued, and appropriated, towards defraying the Expences of defending, protecting, and securing, the British Colonies and Plantations in America: And whereas it is just and necessary, that Provision be made for raising a further Revenue within Your Majesty's Dominions in America, towards defraying the said Expences: We, Your Majesty's most dutiful and loyal Subjects, the Commons of Great Britain in Parliament assembled, have

4 a 2

Top left: The British secretary of state for America, Henry Seymour Conway.

Top right: New York's lieutenant governor, Cadwallader Colden. *Courtesy of* Harper's Encyclopedia of United States History, *Harper & Brothers, 1905.*

Left: Few in the British government appreciated the furor that the 1768 passage of the Stamp Act inspired in America. *Courtesy of the Library of Congress.*

Parliament reasoned, the colonists also benefited from this military action and therefore ought to help with the tab.

But the issue here in America wouldn't be *what* but *how.*

The Parliament in London—a government some three thousand miles across an ocean, in which the colonists had no representation—had basically just told the Americans that, like it or not, you are going to pay us this tax. The colonies, however, all had their own provincial assemblies, and they expected that they would at least have been consulted in the matter. Instead, Parliament bypassed them all and simply made it the new law of the land. But it wasn't entirely capricious. The home-rule provincial assemblies had been making excuses for years as to why they couldn't afford the various military expeditions against the French. Royal governors—the official representatives of His Majesty in the colonies—pushed their imperial agendas against an unending tide of resistance from the local interests represented by the respective assemblies. There was little history to prove that the existing system was going to be any more successful in approving the tax, so there was little point in involving them.

But more than that, there was a distinct fear among many of the powers in London that Americans—those provincial, backwater bumpkins—would soon outnumber the population back home. And it wasn't an entirely unreasonable fear. England was, after all, an island with only so many square miles and so many resources. By comparison, North America was vast, with plenty of room for the colonists to grow into and abundant natural resources to fuel that growth. And, in 1765, with the French removed as a barrier against them moving into the interior of the continent, there was little to stop it. (There were, of course, the Native Americans, but European interests viewed them as, ultimately, no match for their armies.) If the center of gravity shifted across the ocean, what would that mean for the traditional British power culture?

The analogy has often been made characterizing the relationship between England and America as that of parent and child. A more accurate analogy, however, might be the dynamic between master and servant. England created the colonies in North America, as elsewhere, for one purpose only—the enrichment of England. Colonies were always to be subservient to the interests of the Mother Country. England was the master and America the servant, whose station in life was to make the world more comfortable and profitable for the master. A master could never suffer to permit a servant to think himself equal. Such folly would just upset the natural, God-given order of things!

By this point, the colonists had been in America for several generations and had managed to carve from the wilderness considerable swaths of European-style civilization. Settlers in these areas were no longer limited to living hand-to-mouth existences while clinging to the peripheries of the empire. A distinctly "American" culture was evolving. Yes, they were still subjects of the king—and proud of it, thank you very much—but they had a somewhat elevated self-image. They saw themselves as an integral part of the empire but also as an equal partner in the enterprise—as equal possessors of the same rights and deserving of the same respect as anyone born on the island nation proper. As a matter of economics, politics and cultural preservation, many of the folks back in London had other ideas as to just where these Americans fit into the imperial scheme of things—and it certainly wasn't right alongside themselves. For them, to back down on the Stamp Act would be as good as an admission that the Americans were their equals and that a provincial assembly should enjoy the same respect as an equal of Parliament—that the servant was the equal of the master.

Both sides would dig in their heels over this one.

In broad terms, this was a case of that well-worn phrase, "no taxation without representation." In political and legal terms, however, it was a little more complex than this slogan conveyed. In reality, by virtue of their assemblies, Americans enjoyed a greater degree of representation and voting rights than their English counterparts. Thanks to the Mother Country's more strident prerequisites of property ownership, it was estimated at the time that a full 75 percent of England's adult males did not have *any* real representation in any standing forum of governance. Nevertheless, so those in power argued, Parliament was bound to represent the interests of *everyone* in the empire, regardless of whether they were technically, physically represented or not. The Americans—like others even at home—were represented "virtually."

RIOTS

As such details were being argued in the halls of power on both sides of the Atlantic, it did little to assuage the folks out of whose pockets this new tax was to come. Colonial assemblies created committees to address the problem and file the proper protests. Others, however, egged on by the Sons of Liberty and like groups, saw a more effective tool in mob action and took to the streets. It seems no one really appreciated just how worked up people

Benjamin Franklin as painted
by Joseph-Siffred Duplessis
around 1785. *Courtesy of
the National Portrait Gallery,
Smithsonian Institution; gift of the
Morris and Gwendolyn Cafritz
Foundation.*

were about to become. Much of their aggression would find focus on those
who volunteered to act as "stamp agents"—those who collected the tax and
distributed the stamped paper. That even the more politically and socially
astute misread how bad things were about to get is demonstrated by none
other than Benjamin Franklin, who recommended his friend John Hughs for
such a post. Colonists who accepted the post in anticipation of the act's start
that November 1 found themselves the target of angry mobs.

Boston was the first to see outright rioting, on August 14, 1765. Would-be
Massachusetts stamp agent Andrew Oliver was forced to resign the post in
public. Once word spread that the tactic of threatened violence had worked,
mobs became emboldened and sought to settle long-simmering scores against
unpopular political and civic leaders—often for reasons that had nothing
to do with the Stamp Act. Massachusetts lieutenant governor Thomas
Hutchinson—never a very popular man though in power for nearly two
decades—found his family turned out of their home and their possessions
looted or destroyed. When the ringleaders were arrested, local merchants
sympathetic to their cause threatened even more riots and destruction,
forcing their release.

With Boston's example, sometimes the mere hint of violence was enough to send stamp agents running. The Sons of Liberty had developed an efficient network of communication, and word spread quickly. They were soon putting pressure on local merchants and even judges to make use of non-stamped paper as an outright defiance of the law. Portsmouth, New Hampshire; Annapolis, Maryland; Wilmington, Delaware; New Bern, North Carolina; Charleston, South Carolina; and Philadelphia, Pennsylvania, all saw virulent demonstrations.

In New York City, however, it was particularly bad. As the chief port for the northern colonies, it was here that the stamped paper was to be landed and sent on to the agents—assuming any were left. When the ships arrived on October 14, signs were found throughout the city anonymously warning "the first man that either distributes or makes use of stamped paper let him take care of his house, person, and effects." New York's agent, James McEvers, had resigned back in August, after the example of what took place in Boston. By the end of October, merchants had banded together to enact what would be their strongest weapon—nonimportation. They would refuse to deal in merchandise imported from England until the act was repealed— and woe be to the merchant who dared violate the boycott. Lists of those merchants who had signed the pledge were printed in newspapers, and these men were hailed as patriots.

The politicians who were plying the normal channels would prove ineffective. Violent protests would soon burn themselves out and only inspired further entrenchment in London. By hurting English merchants through nonimportation, however, those same merchants would be forced to petition their representatives in Parliament—*they* had representation—to consider repeal.

Nevertheless, for the moment, violence would seize New York for four fraught days as mobs that even the Sons of Liberty had a hard time controlling roamed the streets. "But on the evening of the first day of this Month," Colden lamented to Conway on November 5, 1765, "the Mob began to collect together, and after it became dark they came up to the Fort Gate with a great number of Torches, and a Scaffold on which two Images [effigies] were placed, one to represent the Governor in his grey hairs, & the other the Devil by his side."

The grey-haired figure was meant to represent Colden, then seventy-seven years old, with Satan whispering in his ear. The crowds seemed content to curse and shoot at this effigy, but as they drew closer to Fort George's gates, the lieutenant governor must have wondered if their appetite might soon crave the real thing. "This scaffold with the images," a besieged Colden told Conway, "was brought up within 8 or 10 feet of the Gate with the grossest ribaldry from the Mob. As they went from the gate they broke open my coach house, took my charriot [*sic*] out of it & carryed [*sic*] it round the town with the Immages [*sic*] & returned to the Fort Gate, from whence they carryed them to an open place, where they had errected [*sic*] a Jibblett [*sic*], within 100 yards of the Fort Gate & there hung up the Immages. After hanging some time they were burnt in a fire prepared for the purpose, together with my charriott, a single horse chair and two sledges, our usual carriages when snow is on the ground, which they took out of my Coach house."

Like a fancy car in modern times, a personal carriage—particularly ones as grand as Colden had—was a status symbol. Trashing them was as much about symbolic insult as wanton vandalism. "While this was doing," Colden reported, "a great number of gentlemen of the Town if they can be call'd so, stood around to observe the outrage on their King's Governor."

As the mob passed the fort, they taunted the soldiers with words, bricks and stones as they beat on the walls, daring them to open fire. They were outnumbered several hundred to around 130. Major Thomas James maintained strict discipline. His restraint, however, was rewarded by the mob breaking into his house, destroying his belongings and burning it to the ground—as well as, according to Colden, "threatening to take away his life in the most shamefull [*sic*] manner."

By 9:30 p.m., the mob began to disperse on its own, leaving a city in shock and disarray.

INFLAMMATORY PAPERS

When Colden wrote Conway that things had quieted down, he was likely hoping that the mob's energies had been spent and he could, quietly, at last get the stamped paper offloaded from the ship sitting in the port. But, he also added, "the inflammatory Papers continue to be published, exciting the People to oppose the execution of the Act of Parliament for laying a Stamp Duty in the Colonies. The most remarkable of these Papers is inclosed [*sic*]."

Newspapers, signs and broadsides had been distributed, urging the people to rise up against the act. The newspaper he included with his dispatch to Conway bore the masthead of the *Constitutional Courant*, and "remarkable" was putting it mildly. Its debut issue, dated September 21, 1765, featured the segmented snake cartoon, each piece representing a colony, with the caption below reading "JOIN or DIE." It was the revival of a graphic device Benjamin Franklin had used in his *Pennsylvania Gazette* for May 9, 1754, when he hoped to rally the colonies to their common defense on the eve of the last French and Indian War. The introduction topping the first column promised an incendiary read:

> *To the PUBLIC. When a new public Paper makes its appearance, the reader will naturally be curious to know from whence it came, the publisher, and the design of it. To gratify that curiosity, know reader, that the publisher having formerly acquired a competent knowledge of the Printing-business, for his amusement furnished himself with a set of proper materials;—and the authors of the following pieces having been acquainted him that they applied to the printers in York, who refused to publish them in their news-papers—not because they disapproved them, or were apprehensive of danger, but purely because several of their friends had been anxious on their account; and particularly desired them to be careful not to publish any thing that might give the enemies of liberty an advantage; which they would be glad to take, over them; and as these pieces are thought to be wrote with greater freedom than any thing that has yet appeared in the public prints, they thought proper to shew [sic] so much complaisance to the advice of their friends, as to desire to be excused, and to return the copies: But I, who are under no fear of disturbing either friends or enemies, was pleased with the opportunity of turning my private amusements to the public good; I not only undertook to publish them, but now inform my countrymen, that I shall occasionally publish any thing else that falls in my way, which appears to me to be calculated to promote the cause of Liberty, of virtue, of religion and my country, of love and reverence to its laws; and constitution, and unshaken loyalty to the King———And so I bid you heartily farewell.*
>
> *Andrew Marvell.*

What followed the introduction did not disappoint. The emotional grandstanding was taken up by an author under the name "Philoleutherus."

> *At a time when our dearest privileges are torn from us, and the foundation of all our liberty subverted, every one who has the least spark of love to his country, must feel the deepest anxiety about our approaching fate. The hearts of all who have a just value for freedom, must burn within them; when they see the chains of abject slavery just ready to be riveted about their necks.*

The *Constitutional Courant* made use of the "Join or Die" snake cartoon attributed to Benjamin Franklin. It was used here to signify unity among the colonies against the Stamp Act.

With the tone set, Philoleutherus asserted, "It has been undeniably demonstrated...that no Englishman can be taxed, agreeable to known principles of our constitution, but by his own consent, given either by himself or his representatives...these colonies are not in any sense at all represented in the British parliament."

The English colonies in North America were established under royal charters, or concessions, that guaranteed that the rights of the colonists as Englishmen would be preserved. Philoleutherus contended that "the tremendous conclusion, therefore, forces itself upon us, that the public faith of the nation...is violated, and we robbed of our dearest rights by the late law erecting a stamp-office among us."

Angered by London's obstinate refusal to even hear the colonists' grievances, Philoleutherus lamented, "Poor America, the bootless privilege of complaining, always allowed to the vilest criminals on the rack, is denied thee!"

But Philoleutherus saved his strongest invective for those who would support the Stamp Act: "Ye blots and stains of America! Ye vipers of human kind! Your names shall be blasted with infamy, the public execration shall persue [*sic*] you while living, and your memories shall rot, when death has disabled you from propagating vassalage and misery further."

The second of the two essays, penned by "Philopatriæ," was perhaps more thoughtful though no less stinging. He opened by countering the view that those who oppose the Stamp Act are all supporters of the violence just seen in Boston. He asserted when news of the riots arrived in New York, "On the contrary, they hear of them with concern and sorrow."

The theme of potential slavery was repeated: "Let us not flatter ourselves, that we shall be happier, or treated with more lenity than our fellow slaves in Turkey; human nature is the same every where [*sic*], and unlimited power is as much to be dreaded among us, as it is in the most barbarous nations on earth: It is slavery that hath made them barbarous, and the same cause will have the same effect upon us."

Philopatriæ attacked the problem of the apparent social and ideological distance between the members of Parliament and the colonies from an interesting angle. Politicians in England who ran for office were required to have "considerable property in England." While restricting office to wealthy landowners might seem rather unfair to modern eyes, there was a certain logic to it. Such an arrangement meant that the politician's fortunes would be tied to those of the community who lived on his land. "But consider this rule with respect to America," Philopatriæ asked. "Have all the members of parliament property there? Will they each feel part of the burdens they lay upon us?—No. But their own burdens will be lightened by laying them upon our shoulders, and all they take from us will be gains to themselves: Heaven defend us from such representatives!"

Both authors expressed their undying loyalty to the King, preferring to lay blame anywhere but on his head. To do otherwise would have been an outrage even Philoleutherus would not attempt. "We cherish the most unfeigned loyalty to our rightful sovereign," he declared; "we have a high veneration for the British parliament; we consider them as the most august assembly on earth; but the wisest of kings may be misled...Be assured, my countrymen, whatever spirit we manifest on this juncture, it cannot be offensive to our sovereign: He glories in being King of freemen, and not of slaves."

While asserting similar allegiances, Philopatriæ nevertheless proved the more radical—and prophetic. "If she [England] would strip us of all the advantages derived to us from the English constitution, why should we desire to continue our connection?" he asked. "We might as well belong to France, or any other power; none could offer a greater injury to our rights and liberties than is offered by the Stamp Act."

It is that sentiment that no doubt gave the likes of Colden reason for anger and concern. These were strong words indeed. Nothing like them had been publicly printed before. And, being aimed at powerful people, these papers brought with them no small amount of personal danger to those who wrote them.

And to those who published them.

PRINTERS

The printers in New York at the time would have been Hugh Gaine, William Weyman and John Holt. Historian of the American press Isaiah Thomas wrote, "Gaine's political creed, it seems, was to join the strongest party." Indeed, his allegiance would shift in the coming decade. But in 1764 and 1765, he was doing printing for the assembly and would likely have shunned anything so controversial as the pieces apparently being proffered. Weyman had suspended his *Gazette*, so he had no newspaper in which to print the pieces even if he wanted to.

John Holt was another matter.

Rather than retreat from the Stamp Act, he would continue to issue his *Post-Boy* after November 1—the date the act took effect—with the declaration that it stood for "LIBERTY and PROSPERITY, and no STAMPS." He no doubt had planned this open challenge to the authorities even as early as September, as he had become the darling of the Sons of Liberty and enjoyed their protection. It is difficult to say if he would have turned down the job, no matter how virulent the polemics were. It is also possible that with only two active printers in New York, the identity of "Andrew Marvell" could hardly remain a secret for long. Mr. Marvell had to print outside of the city.

"This was distributed along the Post Roads by the Post Riders," Colden explained to Conway. "I examined the Post Master [of New York, who happened to be Colden's son, Alexander] in this place to know how this came to be done. He assured me that it was without his knowledge: That he had examined the Post Riders and found that one or more Bundles of them were delivered at Woodbridge, New Jersey, to the Post Rider, by James Parker Secrettary [*sic*] to the General Post Office in N. America. Parker was formerly a printer in this place and has now a Printing Press and continues to print occasionally. It is believed that this Paper was printed by him."

Such a revelation must have come as a surprise to Colden. He had known James Parker from his days as the King's printer in New York and hired him to print his book on gravity—the first work of physics ever printed in America. There is evidence that the two families were at least somewhat friendly. Could it be that Parker, an otherwise upright subject, had joined the ranks of the miscreants who threatened the peace of Colden's province?

Before he made his report to Conway, Colden had written to Parker's old friend and silent business partner, Benjamin Franklin, on October 1. "My regard to you makes me give you the trouble of the inclosed Printed Paper," he told him, "one or more bundles of which, I am well informed were deliever'd to the Post Rider at Woodbridge by James Parker, were distributed by the Post Riders in several parts of this Colony, and I believe likewise in the Neighboring Colonies: the doing of which was kept Secret from the Post Master of this Place. It is believed that this Paper was Printed by Parker after the Printers in this Place had refused to do it, perhaps you may be able to judge from the Types. As he is Secrettary [*sic*] to the General Post Office in America, I am under a necessity of takeing [*sic*] notice of it to the Secrettary of State [Conway] by the return of the Packet which is daily expected, and I am unwilling to do this without giving you previous notice by a Merchant Ship which Sails Tomorrow."

JAMES PARKER

Born in Woodbridge, New Jersey, in 1714, James Parker was apprenticed to the pioneering printer William Bradford in New York in 1725. Parker's father, Samuel, had died and his mother, Jana, took care of the paperwork. Bradford was a good choice—he had been Philadelphia's first printer and published New York's first newspaper. When, in 1733, Bradford found he didn't have enough work to keep Parker busy, however, he elected to offer the remaining eight months of the indenture for sale. Part of the agreement was Bradford had to pay to feed and keep Parker—so when business was slow, he became a liability. By that point, Parker was nineteen years old and likely felt he was good enough to start making his own way in the world. Before Bradford could sell his services, James Parker ran away.

Apprentices ran away for any number of reasons, including abusive masters. There is no indication this was the case here. But so long as he was, in effect, a "wanted man," Parker couldn't remain in New York. Bradford offered a reward for the return of his wayward apprentice in his newspaper. The closest place a new printer could find work would have been Philadelphia—and it was there young Parker appears to have gone. He ended up working in the shop of Benjamin Franklin, the beginning of what was to become a lifelong friendship.

By the 1740s, Franklin entertained ambitions to become a proper gentleman in the English style—this was before the coming revolution would make an American out of him. And that meant he couldn't continue to get his hands dirty as a printer. He began to form partnerships with up-and-coming printers, bankrolling their shops for a cut of the profits. He evidently saw talents worth backing in Parker because in 1742 he sent him back to New York with a silent partnership, financing Parker's establishment of a printing shop of his own. He saw him as the heir apparent to the aging William Bradford's dominance in the New York trade.

Parker would indeed become a major force in New York's literary evolution. His newspaper, the *New-York Gazette and Weekly Post-Boy*, would become the paper of record. He was named the official government printer for both the King and the local governments, and his clients included the city's elite.

Around 1752, after a turbulent period printing the rabble-rousing periodical the *Independent Reflector* in New York for a trio of reformist lawyers (including later New Jersey governor William Livingston), he set his sights back on New Jersey. Up until then, those in the province who needed printing would go either to New York or Philadelphia, whichever was more convenient. Even the provincial government went outside the colony. New Jersey was divided into East and West Jersey, with co-capitals at Perth Amboy (East) and Burlington (West). For printing, Perth Amboy went to New York and Burlington to Philadelphia. Occasionally, when the government needed to print money, by law it needed to be done inside the colony, under supervision. Printers had been required to haul their equipment into New Jersey from outside to do such jobs and then remove it again when done. As Parker's native Woodbridge was just north of Perth Amboy, it was obvious that he could offer his services more conveniently to East Jersey (plans for a Burlington shop would fail in part, ironically, because of the Stamp Act). His new printing office in Woodbridge would be the first permanent print shop in New Jersey.

GODDARD

There is no evidence to suggest that Franklin ever pursued the *Constitutional Courant* issue with Parker. He probably didn't have the time to make a study of the print to determine if it had, indeed, come from Parker's press.

In the end, however, most historians have concluded that it was not James Parker who printed the *Constitutional Courant*. In Isaiah Thomas's 1810 work *The History of Printing in America*, he tells that the paper "was printed by William Goddard, at Parker's printing house in Woodbridge, Goddard having previously obtained Parker's permission occasionally to use his press."

The significance of this statement was explained by historian Ralph Frasca—perhaps the only historian to make a detailed study of the question regarding who really printed the paper. Thomas and Goddard were close friends, he explained, and Goddard assisted him in preparing the second edition of his book (which would not be published until after Thomas's death in 1874). In his proofreading, Goddard pointed out to Thomas that he had mistakenly called the paper the *Constitutional Gazette* and informed him it had indeed been printed in Woodbridge. He did not refute the statement that he had been its printer. Furthermore, in a private letter to Thomas, Goddard admitted responsibility outright. He told him that John Holt "showed me several elegantly written and highly spirited essays, against the unjust tax, which no printer in New-York dared publish. I volunteered my services, went to Woodbridge, and obtained leave to use the apparatus there at pleasure, where I planned a newspaper with this title."

Born in New London, Connecticut, Goddard was the son of Dr. Giles Goddard, who served as the town's postmaster. The younger Goddard served an apprenticeship under James Parker in New York from 1755 to 1761. The

William Goddard is believed to have printed the *Constitutional Courant* on James Parker's press at Woodbridge, New Jersey.

next year brought a chance to go to Providence, Rhode Island, to start that colony's first newspaper. The governor, Stephen Hopkins (who would go on to sign the Declaration of Independence), backed Goddard's *Providence Gazette and Country Journal* as a propaganda outlet for his political views. It was printed "at the Sign of Shakespeare's Head," referring to the sign under which he traded, which featured William Shakespeare's portrait. Ralph Frasca believed that this was significant, as the *Constitutional Courant* was published "at the Sign of the Bribe refused," reminiscent of Goddard's advertising device.

In spite of this encouraging start, Goddard's fortunes in Rhode Island were not as promising as he had hoped. On May 11, 1765, he was forced to cease publication of his *Gazette* due to a lack of subscribers and advertisers. The impending Stamp Act likely hastened his decision. He had tried to gain the province's government printing to no avail—that was all sewn up by Benjamin Franklin's sister-in-law, Ann Franklin. About this time, Goddard decided to return to New York, leaving the print shop to his mother, Sarah (who, along with Ann Franklin, was among the several unsung women who operated print shops when the original male owners were absent for various reasons). There, he found employment with John Holt, whom he knew from when they both worked for Parker. He would make several return trips to Providence, including one where he re-issued his *Gazette* for one *Providence Gazette Extraordinary* edition on August 24 to rail against the Stamp Act. Such strong anti-act sentiments and his associations with Holt in New York—and by default Parker—are strong bits of further supporting evidence that he was indeed behind the *Constitutional Courant*.

Assuming it was indeed William Goddard behind the name "Andrew Marvell," it was an interesting choice of pseudonym. Andrew Marvell (1621–1678) was a real person and a member of Parliament during the reign of Charles II. Marvell opposed the King by supporting a republican government following the Restoration.

But what about Alexander Colden's claim to his father that it was James Parker—secretary and comptroller of the post office—who turned the bundles over to the postrider? The younger Colden learned this from the rider, so the question is whether the rider knew Parker by sight. If he didn't know his face, either he merely assumed it was Parker, when it was actually Parker's son, Samuel Franklin Parker, or Goddard misled him into thinking *he* was Parker. But if the rider knew Parker and received the bundles from his hands, two possibilities emerge—either Parker didn't know what they contained or else he was secretly in on Goddard's plan to distribute the vitriolic publication on some level.

Parker had a plausible alibi, however. Correspondence around the time in question places him in Burlington, New Jersey. He had opened a new shop there and would have issued New Jersey's first newspaper had it not been for the Stamp Act. Another reason he abandoned the effort was a new law that required him, as secretary and comptroller for the post office, to live in New York—never mind that he could have easily done the job anywhere. So what about it? Was he in Burlington when he was alleged to have been handing off these papers to the postrider? The answer seems to lie in the interpretation of a single word.

On September 22, 1765, James Parker wrote a letter to Benjamin Franklin, dated from Burlington, with the added note that it was a Sunday night. In it, he discussed matters pertaining to the new rates tables he would have to print for the post office. Indeed, he would be departing for Woodbridge the next day to do so. In the next paragraph, however, Parker informed Franklin, "I wrote you about a Fortnight ago, via New-York; but whether it went by a Vessel bound to Liverpool, or whether Mr. Colden kept it till this Packet I know not." A fortnight equals two weeks, which would place the mailing of this other letter around September 8.

The question, however, rests on the phrase "via New-York" and, specifically, on the word "via."

In the strictest definition of the word, "via" means "by way of." Parker could have sent his letter from Burlington to New York to be forwarded to Franklin. Evidently it passed through Alexander Colden's hands. However, the editors of *The Papers of Benjamin Franklin*, volume 12, published in 1968, seem to have taken a different meaning. They stated, "Parker wrote Franklin, September 22, that he had enclosed this new account [of Franklin's accounting with David Hall] in a letter sent *from* [italics added] New York 'about a Fortnight ago,' that is, about September 8, but neither that letter nor any acknowledgment from Franklin has been found."

This is important because if the letter was written and mailed *from* New York, it would put Parker on the side of New Jersey closer to Woodbridge at the critical time. If the September 8 letter were ever found, and if Parker continued his habit of including the location as well as the date, it would answer the question. But, alas, the letter seems to be lost.

Whether Parker played a role in the *Constitutional Courant* or not, he was in a difficult spot—*he* was the one getting in trouble with Cadwallader Colden, not Goddard or the essayists. Fortunately for him, Colden's governor's council appears to have been too jittery to act. "The Gentlemen of the Council think it prudent at this time to delay making more particular inquiry," Colden told

Conway in his October 12, 1765 report, "lest it should be the occasion of raising the Mob which it is thought proper by all means to avoid."

James Parker was a "law and order" kind of man. Throughout his life, he was possessed of a strong and abiding sense of duty. On the surface, he was about as good a candidate for a Loyalist as one might find. And yet, he also had friends amongst the Sons of Liberty and in the last year of his life would become embroiled in controversy for having printed a broadside for one of its leading lights, Alexander McDougall. When the petty bureaucracy of London resulted in complicated delays of his pay for various government positions, his expressions of tried patience made him sound as if he might be a breath away from joining the radicals. Did he feel some empathy—if not sympathy—for the frustrations his fellow Americans were laboring under? Was this once proud subject of the King beginning to question his loyalty?

We will never know. On July 2, 1770, death spared him the agonizing choices that circumstances would shortly force upon his neighbors.

Garden State Legacy #12, June 2011

CHAPTER 6

Newark Airport

Where Aviation Became an Industry

I have to smile sometimes when I hear people complaining about airlines. Yes, there are reasons to be unhappy. But then again, consider exactly what it is they do every day, all over the world, in all sorts of weather and, by and large, with great safety: operate complex machines that can hurtle you at hundreds of miles per hour through the sky, over mountains, across continents and oceans and then land you gently on the ground somewhere else in a fraction of the time it would take via any other means of transportation.

It's really saying something when we've become so jaded by this fact that we can whine about the size of our bag of peanuts.

That we have the luxury of considering the act of flying so routinely is thanks, in part at least, to New Jersey. Aviation may have been born at Kitty Hawk, North Carolina, but it matured into an industry in Newark.

BADER AND HADLEY

When Europeans first began arriving in North America, they quickly understood that Hudson's Bay was going to be important. In addition to sheltered ports for transatlantic ships, rivers offered access to the interiors of the Northeast. And settlement at the southern tip of Manhattan Island was just the start of it. Expansion gave rise to Newark, Jersey City, Elizabeth and other communities over in New Jersey, and a spreading web of roads, highways, canals and railroads made the region a transportation nexus.

By the time aircraft had been added to that mix, the New Jersey and New York metro area was among the most logical locations for an airfield. That meant that a variety of aviation firsts ended up happening in the Garden State—some even long before powered flight.

The earliest event dates back to January 9, 1793. Jean Pierre Blanchard launched a hot air balloon—the first in the Americas—from Philadelphia, sailing across the Delaware River some fifteen miles, before landing in Deptford Township, New Jersey. Among those to watch the spectacle from what was then the nation's capital were President George Washington and four future presidents: John Adams, Thomas Jefferson, James Madison and James Monroe.

Then, on November 20, 1818, another Frenchman by the name of Louis Charles Guille took off in his own hot air balloon, this time from Jersey City. At about five hundred feet off the ground, no doubt to the thrill and no small concern of anyone below him, he cut the lines holding his basket to the balloon. What saved him from crashing to the ground was a parachute—believed to have been the very first use of such a thing in America.

When it came to powered flight, New Jersey featured in the origins of a rather fundamental part of the aviation lexicon. The word "air-port" first appeared in a 1919 newspaper, used by Robert Woodhouse. He was describing Bader Field at Atlantic City, which was New Jersey's first such dedicated facility for aircraft. It had opened in 1910 and started passenger service the following year. But the term was a hybrid of both "air" in the aviation sense and "port" in the nautical. He was actually referring to Bader Field's seaplane service to New York City—the first in the nation, by the way. The aircraft themselves he described as "flying limousines."

Of course, the name "airport" would stick in the purely aviation sense, but for a long time it would still be more accurate to call them "fields." They were just that—reasonably flat, open spaces, long enough that an airplane could take off and land. According to some who remember these early days, there wasn't really even a designated runway—pilots just took off or landed as the direction of the wind at the moment dictated. Pretty much any unobstructed strip of real estate around five hundred or six hundred feet long would have been adequate for the light airplanes of the era.

Since most aircraft were still rather small, the paying thrill-seeking passenger aside, the idea of economically carrying travelers in any profitable quantity remained impractical. The place where an enterprising aviation company could make some money was in the delivery of the mail. Up to that point, mail moved as fast as men, horses and automobiles could carry it—and given the dismal state of most roads, that wasn't very fast. The railroad and boats could move large quantities but were confined to where rails or waterways led. An airplane, by contrast, could fly quickly and directly between points. The concept of rural free delivery to even the most remote homes had been nationally adopted by 1902, and certainly, this new "airmail" was a good fit.

And here, too, New Jersey would be at the fore.

The U.S. Postal Service was on the hunt for an airfield to act as the New York regional terminus for this new airmail service. It considered Hazelhurst Field—later known as Roosevelt Field—on Long Island but found it too vulnerable to fog. So it started looking west, across the Hudson River into New Jersey. It found a good patch of flat ground in South Plainfield, on seventy-seven acres owned by John R. Hadley, who agreed to lease it to the postal service beginning November 1, 1924. By December 15, lights had been installed, including a revolving beacon rotating six times per minute, and a radio mast. On July 1, more than fifteen thousand people came to watch Dean Smith and J.D. Hill pull their respective airplanes into a moonlit sky to carry sacks of mail on a maiden flight to Cleveland.

They were still working the bugs out of this flying business, however. Mechanical failure forced Smith to turn around almost immediately and return to Hadley for a quick repair—all embarrassingly witnessed by the lingering crowds and newsreel photographers. He was quickly back in the air again, but yet more engine troubles forced him to make an emergency landing near Kylertown, Pennsylvania. Two hours later, he was back in the skies one more time, in a new plane, but ran out of gas just fifteen minutes shy of Cleveland. He crash-landed upside down in a farmer's vineyard. The startled farmer, apparently unfamiliar with the ways of aviators, is said to have looked at the crumpled aircraft and asked Smith, "Do you always land this way?"

By contrast, however, J.D. Hill made it all the way without mishap. All things considered, the post office still deemed it enough of a success that it would continue with the service. On October 1, 1928, the postal service announced the start of international airmail service from Hadley to Mexico and Canada.

Hadley Field no longer exists. By the 1960s, technological advances in aviation had made it obsolete, and residents of the encroaching suburbs didn't like the noise and risk of living next to an airport. The land was sold off to developers in 1968 and is now home to a shopping mall (Hadley Plaza), industrial park and hotel.

NEWARK

With mail delivery still driving aviation as a business proposition, there was a desire to open fields ever closer to the population center of New York City. Newark was prime real estate for such a venture, and in late 1919, local businessmen started collecting public subscriptions toward constructing an airport. They set their sights as high as the aircraft they hoped to see, looking to raise $25,000—not an inconsiderable sum back then—but only managed to get $7,000.

Undaunted, they cleared a field on the edge of the Forest Hill Golf Club and laid down a cinder runway. They dubbed it Heller Field, in honor of a prominent North Newark family who owned a tool factory and were involved in real estate development. Pilot Walter H. Stevens proved true to the old postman's creed, "Neither rain nor snow nor dark of night…" as he left Washington, D.C., in a blinding snowstorm, laden with some seven hundred pounds of mail, and headed for Heller Field on December 6, 1919. A minute shy of two hours later, he safely touched down. But, as subsequent fliers discovered, it wasn't the most ideal of locations. There were trees to dodge and power lines. By May 1920, the post office withdrew its business and the field was closed.

While Heller Field was a failure, it did make some people realize the advantages of an airport near Newark. Then, when the Holland Tunnel project got underway in the mid-1920s, there was a revived interest among Newark's aviation enthusiasts—mail planes landing at a Newark airport in the meadowlands, they argued, would now be just twenty minutes from the city. Finding the political will, however, was difficult. Newark's then mayor, Thomas L. Raymond, was skeptical about investing in a technology that seemed far from perfected. To many sober-minded people, airplanes were novelties that were good for barnstorming entertainment and maybe delivering some mail. But they tended to crash a lot and just didn't seem like something to hang one's financial hat on.

And then Charles A. Lindbergh skittered across Roosevelt Field in his Spirit of St. Louis and on up into the clouds and the history books.

It was May 20, 1927—7:52 a.m. to be precise. In the thirty-three hours that followed, it would have been hard for even the harshest critic of flying not to root for him in his bid to be the first to fly solo across the Atlantic Ocean. When he touched down at Le Bourget Field in Paris, France, he became the poster boy that American aviation sorely needed—a lanky, freckled lad exuding an honest-to-goodness self-effacing farm-boy charm. The notion of this young man, all alone, conquering the divide between the New and Old Worlds through wholesome grit and determination resonated with the American ideal and made him an overnight hero, nicknamed "The Lone Eagle."

Maybe, a few more folks started to wonder, there really *was* something to this flying business after all.

Certainly it changed Mayor Raymond's mind. There is a story that he was shaving one morning about a month after Lindbergh's flight when he had an epiphany, ran downstairs and declared excitedly, "We will build an airport!" The more staid "official" announcement confirmed the influence "Lucky Lindy" had on the mayor: "This young man has demonstrated it is possible to leave one field and reach another thousands of miles away without mishap. We might as well make up our minds to build an airport."

When the Port of New York Authority was scouting potential locations for this new metropolitan airport, Newark ranked ninth out of ten candidates. But in the end, the assistant secretary of commerce for aeronautics—they were now taking aviation seriously enough to give it its own secretary—sent word from Washington, D.C., on July 18, 1927, that Newark would get the prize. In early 1928, a commission appointed by then president Herbert Hoover confirmed that Newark was indeed ideally suited, based on an ability to handle the expected air traffic from the west and south.

The city commission voted to put up a whopping $5.5 million toward the project but hedged its bets by privately reminding investors that even if it all failed, it was still prime real estate for industrial development. Engineers overcame the marshy land with a combination of luck and cleverness. It just so happened that at the same time, Newark Bay's shipping channel was being deepened. So they piped some 1.5 million cubic yards of dredged material the three miles to the airport construction site. Mother Nature, however, fought back, dousing the site with rain a total of thirty-three days, each single soggy day knocking them back another day or two off schedule. But finally, by July, they had a 1,600-foot runway—in itself an aviation first. Runways had been grassy fields or maybe cinder, as at Heller. But at Newark, they added asphalt to the cinder, making a solid, hard, durable surface—the first such runway ever used in the United States.

Sadly, Mayor Raymond would not live to see the dedication of the airport he had banked on for Newark. He died unexpectedly on October 7, 1928, just three days before the opening ceremonies. Instead of a triumphant ribbon-cutting, Newark officials attended his funeral, and the opening was

The Newark marshlands before the building of the airport. *Courtesy of the Newark Public Library.*

A horse-drawn machine was used to create the first runway. *Courtesy of the Newark Public Library.*

pushed back two days. Local department store owner and philanthropist Louis Bamberger cited Newark Airport as among the greatest "monuments of [Raymond's] great public service."

Despite the sad shadow Raymond's death cast, Newark Airport was at last a reality. It was the crowning jewel of the city's efforts to become a major transportation hub, and they mounted aggressive publicity campaigns to generate public interest. It certainly helped when the U.S. government made it its eastern airmail terminal.

But one effort in particular stands out.

GRAF ZEPPELIN

There was still an element of romance to the idea of soaring among the clouds in 1928. The pinnacle of this allure was the civilized luxury offered up by lighter-than-air ships—dirigibles. And "ship" was an apt term. They were growing increasingly bigger, like ocean liners of the sky. The fall of 1928 saw completion of the greatest of them all—the mighty *Graf Zeppelin*.

Germany had invested heavily in the lighter-than-air concept, and its greatest champion was Ferdinand Adolf Heinrich August Graf von Zeppelin. The German aristocrat and military officer first encountered the thrill of flight as a volunteer observer with the Union Army of the Potomac during the Civil War. They used balloons to lift observers aloft. Back in Germany, when he retired from the military at age fifty-two, he devoted his time to developing larger and more sophisticated lighter-than-air ships with his Zeppelin Company. Indeed, the word "zeppelin" became synonymous with the machines themselves.

Personally, he had a good relationship with America, returning to consult with Thaddeus S.C. Lowe,

Ferdinand Adolf Heinrich August Graf von Zeppelin was inspired to build lighter-than-air ships by his experiences in the United States during the Civil War.

the father of aerial military reconnaissance who had helped inspire Zeppelin's own fascination with flight during the war. So it was probably a blessing that he died on March 8, 1917—before the United States entered the war against Germany on April 6. Under the terms of the eventual Treaty of Versailles, the development of zeppelins was halted as part of the overall disarmament. The *Graf Zeppelin,* named after its champion ("Graf" is the German equivalent of "Count"), was a statement of German reassertion as a leader in the field.

And what a statement it was!

At 776 feet long, seeing it in the sky was like watching an ocean liner floating over your house. So when it was announced that it would make its first transatlantic flight to America in October 1928, it created quite the stir on both sides of the ocean. If you didn't live somewhere under the path for a firsthand look, you could still vicariously be part of the trip. In honor of the historic flight, Germany printed special stamps and first day covers. Some sixty-five thousand were purchased and mailed to America as souvenirs.

And that gave the organizers of Newark Airport an idea.

At 7:54 a.m. on October 11, the *Graf Zeppelin* left Friedrichshafen, Germany, and headed for Lakehurst Naval Station in New Jersey. There,

The mighty *Graf Zeppelin* caught the imagination of the public as well as the organizers of the new Newark Airport.

the mail would be transferred to airplanes to be taken north to New York. As it approached the East Coast of the United States, however, officials from Newark Airport sent a special radio dispatch to the *Graf*'s commander, Dr. Hugo Echner, another champion of Germany's lighter-than-air ship development. The message informed him that if he were to drop the mail sacks bound for New York with them at Newark instead of at Lakehurst, they would be in the city in just twenty minutes. They didn't receive a reply, however, and the airship arrived as planned at Lakehurst on October 15, 112 hours after it had departed from Germany. Echner and his crew were given a tickertape parade in Manhattan and received invitations to the White House.

It was a good try.

LaGuardia

"NEW JERSEY IS WORLD'S BUSIEST AIRWAY" screamed a headline from the March 13, 1932 *Trenton Sunday Times-Advertiser*. Newark Airport alone was handling more air traffic than London, Paris and Berlin combined—a quarter of the nation's air traffic. The article proclaimed that aviation had become more than the amusement of the rich, emerging as a true industry—and New Jersey was at the forefront. This was, apparently, a realization slow to dawn on the state itself. "Dimly aware that New Jersey had become an aeronautically important State and that the time had come to establish some governmental supervision for the protection of both the public and aviation itself,"

Passengers waiting to board a Ford Tri-Motor aircraft at Newark Airport in 1933. *Courtesy of the Newark Public Library.*

Newark Airport included the first real passenger airline terminal. The faces of these passengers waiting in the lounge in 1933 seem to show mixed emotions! *Courtesy of the Jersey City Free Public Library, the New Jersey Room.*

author Elma Lawson Johnston wrote, "the Legislature last Winter created the New Jersey Aviation Commission." Passenger air travel had by the 1930s at last become a practical—and profitable—venture. Some $50 million was estimated as having been invested in New Jersey's aviation in 1932.

In 1935, Amelia Earhart was on hand to dedicate Newark Airport's new administration building. Everything about it was a monument to aviation as a modern industry. The art deco design epitomized modernity, sleek motion and style—everything the air age promised. But beyond the stylishness were the practical spaces needed for air travel as business. For the first time in the United States—and quite possibly the world—here was a true commercial airline terminal, complete with ticket counter, passenger waiting area, offices and even overnight lodgings for pilots. But it was the glass-enclosed elongated bubble on top that was the real innovation. From within, men could see the whole field, noting the positions of the airplanes coming and going, to control the traffic.

It was the world's first air traffic "control tower."

But the idea of the Garden State cornering a growing market evidently stuck in the craw of some folks over in the Empire State—and perhaps none

Newark Airport celebrated its growth with the dedication of the new administration building on May 16, 1935. *Courtesy of the Jersey City Free Public Library, the New Jersey Room.*

This simple glass enclosure was the first air traffic control tower in history. *Courtesy of the Historic American Buildings Survey/Historic American Engineering Record, the Library of Congress.*

The instrumentation within the Newark Airport control tower. *Courtesy of the Newark Public Library.*

more so than New York City's mayor, the dynamic Fiorello LaGuardia. He had actually thrown a tantrum when his TWA flight landed at Newark when his ticket had said "New York." Refusing to even get off the plane, he demanded that he be taken to Floyd Bennet Field over in Brooklyn. Along the way during this stunt, he told reporters that New Yorkers ought to all get behind the notion of having an airport all their own.

This was more than just the usual (sometimes) good-natured cross-Hudson rivalry. A lot of money was to be had if he could tempt the major carriers to abandon New Jersey for New York. He made a start by securing a deal with American Air Lines to move its terminal from Newark to Bennet Field. Being all the way out in Brooklyn, however, made it less convenient to drive into Manhattan than its Newark competition. Not one to give up easily, LaGuardia was said to have gone so far as to offer police escorts to limousines from Bennet into Manhattan.

Still, LaGuardia had thrown down the gauntlet, and he was prepared to mount a full-bore assault. If Bennet Field wouldn't serve his purposes, he would just build a new airport that would! He, along with American Air

New York's dynamic Fiorello LaGuardia made it a point of his administration to divert the region's air travel to *his* airport in New York. *Courtesy of the Library of Congress, New York World-Telegram & Sun Collection.*

Lines executives from the Bennet Field experiments, began to eye North Beach Airport in Queens as the foundation for a bigger, better facility. Just as Newark had taken advantage of the then-new Holland Tunnel for access into the city, this new field would use the then-new Queens-Midtown Tunnel for the same advantages. Landfill was brought in from Riker Island and put in a metal matrix that to this day bedevils airplane compasses with its magnetic interference. Dedicated on October 15, 1939, as the New York Municipal Airport, its $40 million price tag had many of LaGuardia's critics pronouncing it an expensive boondoggle on New Yorkers. Nevertheless, even before construction began, he was able to leverage the idea to secure commitments from Pan American Airways, American, United, Eastern Air Lines and Transcontinental and Western Air to abandon Newark once completed.

Newark hadn't helped its cause when it insisted on raising the carriers' rent for using their facilities in 1940. One by one, Newark's terminals and hangars began to empty, until shutting it down altogether seemed the only logical choice. Dramatic as it was, the fight for *the* regional airport was just one battle in a larger political, economic and even cultural war between New Jersey and New York for supremacy as the region's transportation nexus. Railroads, for example, had been convinced to offer customers free lighterage at New York Harbor—no extra charge to transfer freight from railcar to warehouse to ship. Jersey City's infamous mayor, Frank "Boss"

Hague, had been arguing for years that it amounted to a subsidy, giving New York an unfair advantage over his own city's waterfronts.

A huge new hangar recently built at Newark Airport to service the largest air transport planes seemed to be obsolete before it opened. Newark's mayor, Meyer C. Ellenstein, even offered it to Hollywood studios to use for soundstages. Yet even this was in response to offers proffered to movie companies by LaGuardia to use land in Queens and Brooklyn for production studios. For the moment, anyway, by attracting the air carriers to Queens, New York had pulled into the lead in the larger, ongoing feud.

LaGuardia may have smelled exploitable political weakness over in Newark. Since 1936, Ellenstein had been under a cloud of indictment on thirty-four counts of conspiracy to buy up Meadowland real estate at inflated prices to expand Newark Airport. After a mistrial, the case against the mayor and seven other officials was heard again on January 6, 1940, but all were acquitted. The accusations had come on the heels of an aviation-related scare for Ellenstein. In April 1936, he received word that the TWA airplane his wife was on had gone missing in an ice storm. She had been on her way to visit their daughters and had been flying a lot at the time, tending to a daughter in St. Louis who had been injured in an auto accident. Mrs.

Newark mayor Meyer Ellenstein fought a running battle with New York mayor LaGuardia over the region's air traffic. *Courtesy of the Newark Public Library.*

Ellenstein had been one of only three survivors out of fourteen when the plane went down near Uniontown, Pennsylvania.

Newark Airport may have been down, but it was not entirely out. Flights from the western United States still landed, and they maintained a twenty-flight-a-day schedule to Washington, D.C. And there were still a lot of people from New Jersey itself who were flying. In an effort to salvage things, Ellenstein turned to another area of the aviation industry. On February 19, 1940, he announced a $35,000-per-year deal with the Brewster Aeronautical Corporation, turning over one of Newark Airport's 175,000-square-foot hangars to be leased as factory space. "The air lines never have been, nor ever will be any direct benefit to a municipality," Ellenstein declared, perhaps not a little as sour grapes. Still, if they wanted to come—and build their own hangars—he certainly wouldn't turn them away. Brewster was abandoning a plant in Long Island City since it was difficult transporting its products to the nearest airport. At Newark, it would be right outside its doors. The United States was still in the grips of the Great Depression at the time, and *any* deal that brought jobs wasn't to be overlooked. Over ten thousand men clogged the roads to Newark Airport to apply for one of the 2,500 positions Brewster announced it would need to fill for the new plant.

Later that month, Ellenstein announced he was even trying to lure the National Air Races, Inc. from Cleveland to Newark. Lowered attendance in Ohio had the race organizers looking for a fresh venue and estimated it would bring over a million spectators. Unfortunately, unable to find sponsors to underwrite the event, Ellenstein was forced to abandon the effort a month later. "I haven't seen any clamor for the races," he admitted. "I guess we may as well forget the whole thing."

Of course, LaGuardia hadn't stolen Newark's business on his own. The federal agency tasked with overseeing such things, the Civil Aeronautics Authority—precursor to the Federal Aviation Authority—had given LaGuardia's new airport an equal status as Newark, paving the way for the shift of terminals. New Jersey senator W. Warren Barbour proposed an investigation of the decision by a Senate Commerce Subcommittee, but the resolution was voted down four to one. It was, of course, a futile effort. It was within the CAA's purview to make such decisions. Nevertheless, there was a feeling in New Jersey that the federal government had dropped the ball in terms of mapping out a long-term program for integrating state-level airport development. State aviation director Gill Robb Wilson would complain later that without such support, New Jersey wasn't prepared to invest in municipal airfields.

Rumors of impropriety over the handling of the contracts and deals that built Newark Airport had not gone away with Ellenstein's acquittal. A House Appropriations Subcommittee investigation of how Works Progress Administration (WPA) money was being spent turned up an alleged connection between David T. Wilentz and a Perth Amboy terra cotta company. Supposedly, the specifications for the façade of one of the hangars had been changed from brick to terra cotta. Some three thousand tiles had been purchased from the company at twenty cents a pop but were never used and ended up in a dump. The problem? David T. Wilentz was New Jersey's attorney general, who had achieved notoriety prosecuting the Lindbergh baby kidnapping case in 1935. And it only got worse. It was also alleged that Wilentz's friends got the contracts for supplying pile-driving equipment and trucks to move the fill dirt.

Wilentz, of course, denied any connections or that any favors had been done. At least in the case of the extra tiles, a plausible explanation was offered by a WPA official. The tiles were surplus and were safely stored *near* a dump and expected to clad a shed for Newark's street cleaning department. But the fact that the allegations were made by New York's representative, John Tabor, demonstrates how nasty this fight was really getting. Aside from the rivalry between the states, there was also politics—Wilentz was a rising star among New Jersey's Democrats, and he accused Tabor, a Republican, of trying to smear him.

True or not, however, the damage had been done. Without the business of the major airlines, Newark's $6 million airport just couldn't survive. American Air Lines' refusal to pay a lease hike and its subsequent heading for LaGuardia was the final straw. New Jersey governor A. Harry Moore tried to salvage things in an eleventh-hour conference with legislative and airline company leaders, all to no avail. It all came down to money. Ellenstein hoped the airlines would at least pay the rest of the $135,000-a-year rent, permitting improvements and expansion. But it was hard to compete when, by contrast, LaGuardia was charging only $73,000. The mayor seemed to feel more than a little betrayed, complaining to reporters that Newark had nursed them when the industry was brand-new and now they were unwilling to bear the expense. He attributed it to unwillingness to pay, not an inability.

On May 28, the Civil Aeronautics Authority declared an inspection of the airfield revealed uneven terrain and hazards to take-off. It's difficult to say how much of this was true and how much was to justify Newark Airport's hastened demise. Governor Moore pleaded with them, claiming a month's stay of execution would permit them to remedy any faults. There was something almost sad and desperate about the whole affair, and in the end, it was in vain.

At midnight on May 30, 1940, after a dozen years ranked among the busiest airports in the world, the air traffic control tower officially closed. The last plane took off at 11:54 p.m., headed for Los Angeles as "a scattering of workmen [and] sightseers watched," reported the *Trenton Evening Times.* "Newark Airport's 13-year career as a giant, pulsating air terminal was over. It had become just a lonely, mud-spotted field for a few charter ships, an oil company, [and] the National Guard."

NATIONAL DEFENSE

The mention of the National Guard is more significant than it might seem. The headlines about the battles between New Jersey and New York were petty compared to those telling of military battles being fought in Europe and the Pacific. Despite the best efforts of the isolationists—including an outspoken Charles Lindbergh—it seemed just a matter of time before

The military has always been part of Newark Airport. This aerial view shows the National Guard's Air Corps. *Courtesy of the Newark Public Library.*

America was embroiled in the expanding war. Mobilization for defense and possible involvement was ongoing, and that included building up air power.

Military aviation had been a part of Newark for some time. An air unit was added to the New Jersey National Guard, which, at the end of October 1928, began leasing five acres from Newark Airport for a dollar a year. And it's worth noting that even at the height of the angst over closing Newark Airport to civil aviation in 1940—just seven days before it was indeed shut down—a small newspaper article announced Staff Sergeant Maurice G. Chevalier of Linden was appointed in charge of the field for the 119th Observation Squadron of the New Jersey National Guard's Air Corps. More to our point, they were based at Newark Airport.

But now those needs would be magnified by the imminent threat of a world war, providing Newark Airport an opportunity to rise to meet them—a grim prospect of an opportunity to be sure, but an opportunity nonetheless.

In fact, it started even before the United States would officially enter the conflict. On the night of June 1—just hours after the last commercial airliner had departed—six planes manufactured by the Stinson Company landed at Newark Airport, destined for the French army. Agents from the Allied nations had come to the United States and were making deals to buy up privately owned airplanes for shipping to Europe.

Moreover, New Jersey as a whole encompassed industries that were vital to the mobilization efforts—factories behind largely unprotected miles of coastline. While Europe was an ocean away, German aircraft carriers could, theoretically at least, bring bombers to those shores. Nazi submarines were known to be prowling the Atlantic. On a trip to Washington, D.C., about funding for waterworks, Governor Moore paid a visit to the War Department. He was seeking help in establishing antiaircraft units in the state—South Jersey's would be headquartered at Atlantic City and North Jersey's at Newark Airport.

The effort met with some success. In July 1940, New Jersey was given its own antiaircraft regiment. By September, the 119th Observation Squadron was training at Newark and the Fort Dix Army base was gearing up to become the region's major training center, further strengthening the state's role in national defense. Throughout the rest of 1940, the legal notices columns in New Jersey's newspapers included announcements seeking bids to perform a variety of construction work at Newark Airport.

Indeed, New Jersey's infrastructure reaped a windfall as the state embraced its newfound role. "Superhighway Through Jersey Vital for Defense" read the front-page headline of the *Trenton Evening Times* for November 10, 1940.

The twenty-mile radius around the city of Newark had seen tremendous industrial growth and, the article maintained, the road system needed upgrading to keep pace. "Today that section of Route 25 between the Holland Tunnel and the Woodbridge Cloverleaf," it declared, "by way of Newark Airport Elizabeth and Linden, is the most congested highway in the world." Rated at 14,000 vehicles per day by the U.S. Bureau of Public Roads as a maximum for safety, the actual number during weekdays was 100,000 and as many as 270,000 on weekends.

In late September, rumor had it that the U.S. Army was seriously considering taking over Newark Airport as a base for bombers. It was even fodder for celebrity and society gossip columnist Dorothy Kilgallen in her "The Voice of Broadway" column, where she described the possibility of the deal resurrecting "the ghost town." The news might have been unwelcome to Governor Moore, however, as he had just appointed a special committee to raise funds to underwrite the reopening of the airport as a privately owned, nonprofit concern. Launched October 2, by the sixteenth it already had $110,000 in the coffers thanks to donations by the Standard Oil Company of New Jersey and—with no small amount of irony—the Port of New York Authority, which kicked in $5,000. They were quick, however, to claim it was "strictly a business proposition," aimed at increasing traffic for their Lincoln and Holland Tunnels.

With perhaps equal irony, what stood in the way of this effort ended up being Newark mayor Meyer Ellenstein, who had been described as "heartbroken" when LaGuardia stole his airport's business. The sticking point was the details of the lease. Ellenstein told reporters in response to the committee's hopes of getting the City Commission's blessings, "They can't jam anything down my throat. I can't give any person or group of persons a blank check on Newark Airport and never intended to."

In January 1941, the Civil Aeronautics Administration (in 1940, the Civil Aeronautics Authority was split into the Civil Aeronautics Administration and the Civil Aeronautics Board) announced that planned improvements would give New Jersey four "Class 3" airports—airports capable of handling existing aircraft of up to fifty thousand pounds gross weight and with runways between 3,500 and 4,500 feet long. Congress had allotted $40,000,000 for beefing up the national aviation capacity, with $1,419,000 going to New Jersey.

But none were "Class 4"—the top grouping, defined by a runway of 4,500 feet or longer and capable of handling the biggest airplanes flying. The only one in the region at the time was LaGuardia in New York. Still, the wartime

Newark Airport saw a large degree of development in response to the Second World War. *Courtesy of the Newark Public Library.*

requirements had pumped needed dollars into developing New Jersey's aviation capacities. President Franklin D. Roosevelt approved $600,000 in WPA money to go into an expansion and needed improvements to Newark Airport.

STACKED

If LaGuardia had allowed himself the pleasure of gloating over his apparent victory at New Jersey's expense, it would have been a case of being careful what you wish for. The neighborhoods around the airport that bore his name had been used to peace and quiet. Now, the drone of airplane prop engines filled the air around 150 times a day, much to the annoyance of an estimated one million New Yorkers. Landlords with properties *not* in the flight paths advertised the fact in bold type in the "for rent" columns. An unnamed naval officer living in Jackson Heights was reported as having started to take photographs of airplanes skimming just above the apartment tops and sending them to LaGuardia, who apparently remained unmoved.

Up until 1940, the airline industry was not yet robust enough to support more than one airport the size of Newark or LaGuardia. But as flying became more of a routine activity, increased demand for flights put more pressure on LaGuardia Airport.

Observers began noticing how inbound airplanes were frequently "stacked," circling the airport waiting for their turn to land. The Associated Press aviation editor, Devon Francis, commented in November 1940 that the "aerial traffic cops" seen in mocking visions of the future from the cartoons might now not be so far-fetched. Seeing the potential danger of the situation, he predicted that Newark Airport would have to be reopened to ease the congestion.

In at least one instance, the dearth of business at Newark had a comical result. Republican dark horse candidate Wendell Wilkie had just lost the 1940 presidential election to Roosevelt. At the end of November, he was flying from Florida to New York for a speaking engagement and landed at Newark so far ahead of schedule that only a handful of the airport's aircraft mechanics were on hand to greet him.

But there was a serious side. Aside from the economic loss and bruised New Jersey pride, the increasing congestion at LaGuardia presented a very real possibility for disaster. In fact, Newark had saved the day back on April 12, 1940. Captain Kit Carson was flying an American Air Lines plane from Buffalo to LaGuardia when he had carburetor troubles in one of his two engines. Limping along on the remaining engine, he managed to land his twenty-one passengers safely at Newark Airport. But had this mishap occurred a little over a month later after it was closed, what would Captain Carson have found? Newark's runways were still there, of course, but no one was maintaining them. An emergency landing in winter, for example, might have found snow and ice obscuring the landing strip. A closer call occurred August 8 with an airplane chartered to take four passengers from Williamsport, Pennsylvania, to LaGuardia. Attempting an emergency landing, the plane crashed a mere three hundred feet from Newark Airport (the cause was not reported). Fortunately, all onboard survived, but one of them had to crawl through the marsh to the National Guard Camp to find help.

Devon Francis had pointed out that it would probably take a fatal collision among the planes stacked over LaGuardia tumbling down into the surrounding residential areas before anyone addressed the problem. New Jersey's vice-chairman of the state planning board, however, was not ready to wait for such a catastrophe. John E. Sloane was outraged by what he saw as the sluggishness with which Newark and Mayor Ellenstein were moving to get Newark Airport reopened. "Criminal negligence will be the verdict," he declared, "if because of congestion in the air over LaGuardia Field there should be an accident to two passenger planes someday. The fault will not be hard to find. It will lie with the people of Newark, Essex County and New Jersey for not insisting vocally that Newark Airport be opened immediately." At the very least, he argued, it could be opened right away for emergency landings.

In January 1941, Sloane took direct aim at Ellenstein's rejection of the fundraising efforts to turn the airport into a nonprofit private entity. "You have rejected the unselfish efforts of citizens and taxpayers to aid Newark in this situation," he wrote the mayor in a pointed letter. "I am sure you are not interested in having this important situation hogtied with peanut politics."

RESURRECTION

Newark made good use of the WPA funds. By April, the Civil Aeronautics Administration declared Newark Airport once again fit for use—if the airlines wanted to come back, that was. On April 15, nine men, working in shifts, climbed back into the control tower, and just like that, Newark Airport was back in business, without fanfare.

That there was so little made of the reopening is surprising on many levels. It was campaign season in Newark, and this was good news Mayor Ellenstein could have used. Newark's Jewish community was proud that one of their own was in the office. The *Jewish Chronicle* backed him, lauding him as "The Fighting Mayor," noting how "the word defeat is not in the dictionary of Ellenstein." But it was, evidently, not enough. Ellenstein lost reelection to Vincent J. Murphy, who seems to have harbored no ill will toward the Jews who had backed his rival, naming eight Jewish citizens to various appointments in the city.

By the end of May, American Air Lines had announced a schedule of twenty-seven flights per day from Newark Airport. Along with American, Eastern, United and TWA had all signed new leases. On June 2, 1941, at 9:20 a.m., an Eastern Air Lines "sleeper" plane touched down to pick up passengers for the first run to Miami. Later that summer, Eastern Air Lines was running half-page newspaper ads declaring, "Now—The Great Silver Fleet Maintains Regular Schedules from Newark Airport!" The return to Newark was said to have been "in the interest of National Defense…enabling you to save precious hours of travel time, to rush emergency shipments via Air Express, and to send important papers overnight to any part of the Country by Air Mail."

Newark Airport was back in business.

On June 3, it got a new manager, Colonel Edwin E. Aldrin, appointed by Governor Charles E. Edison. These were some heavyweight families. The governor was the son of inventor Thomas A. Edison, and Colonel Aldrin was the father of Edwin E. "Buzz" Aldrin Jr.—age eleven at the time of his father's appointment—who would become the second man to walk on the moon after Neil Armstrong on Apollo 11.

A humorous incident, at least in hindsight, happened with Colonel Aldrin's brand-new personal airplane later that year in November. Long before airport security as we know it, a seventeen-year-old boy used to wander around the hangars and admire the aircraft. Sentry Wallace Cook was tasked with guarding the colonel's plane, but while he was at the far end of the hangar, he turned to find the boy eagerly pushing the plane out onto the field! He was chased into the meadows and not seen again, though he wouldn't have gotten very far anyway—the colonel confirmed the plane had no fuel.

Among those happy to see Newark Airport's reopening was Peter M. Schweitzer. He lived in New York, near LaGuardia, and worked in New Jersey, not far from Newark. Mr. Schweitzer decided it would be more convenient to pay the extra forty cents for a round-trip airplane ticket over the tolls at the tunnels and fly as an aerial commuter! The cost of his fifteen-minute flight?

$3.40!

BREWSTER

Mobilization meant lucrative government contracts for companies like the Brewster Aeronautical Corporation. But profits were threatened by a minor mishap that could have been far worse. On August 11, 1941, Brewster test pilot Carl Lansing was bringing in a recently completed navy fighter for a landing at Newark when the landing gear got stuck in the retracted position. He had to circle for two hours and fifteen minutes to burn off enough of the 130 gallons of fuel to lessen the chances of a fiery crash landing. With two fire engines, two ambulances and two rescue and police units at the ready, Lansing brought the plane in, balanced it on the one wheel for a few hundred feet and then dropped it on the right wing, which spun it around a few times, but he stepped out of the cockpit unharmed.

Yet another stuck landing gear mishap occurred the next month, on September 2. Woodward Burke, another Brewster pilot, took off from Newark in a $2 million SB 2A-1 dive bomber for a test flight. Just five seconds off the ground, he realized the gear was jammed and had to spend the next five hours burning off fuel before successfully skidding to a stop with only scrapes to the underside and bent propeller blades.

Brewster had been providing much-needed employment for area workers—as long as you were white. The federal Office of Production Management, through its Negro Employment and Training branch, had touted Brewster as among the employers where color barriers were being broken because they had hired a crew of Negro sheet metal workers. But the National Association for the Advancement of Colored People (NAACP) begged to differ. Five African Americans had been hired only as assistants, and one seemed to have been subsequently fired. The NAACP maintained that this was a token effort, offering three affidavits attesting to Brewster refusing to hire Negro workers. The most flagrant example was at their Long Island City plant, where Edmund Van Osten, a black man from Brooklyn, was told there were no openings for sheet metal workers, only to see the interviewer hire between thirty-five to forty white men for that same job. When Van Osten then applied for the job of an assistant, the interviewer came out and admitted that his men didn't like working "with coloreds."

NEW GLORY

Though Newark had been officially opened since June 1, it saved the party for September. "Once the world's busiest, Newark Airport basked in new glory today after its official reopening caused a traffic jam the likes of which Newark police hope they never see again," said the *Trenton Evening Times* in the September 15 edition. The celebration included an air show that beleaguered police estimated drew over 500,000 people in seventy-five thousand vehicles. They started arriving at dawn, and by 3:00 p.m., Route 25 was backed up to the Holland Tunnel in Jersey City and northbound was bumper-to-bumper up through Elizabeth and Linden. Those unable to get onto the airfield climbed surrounding rooftops to get a glimpse of the private and military craft, stunt fliers and even a 1910 Curtiss Pusher. The paper gushed all the stats—600

Newark police resources were stretched to their limits by the vehicles and crowds that showed up for the 1941 airshow. *Courtesy of the Newark Public Library.*

takeoffs and landings, 750 Newark cops, 400 soldiers—it was like the good old days. Unfortunately, the event was marred by injuries (seventy-five cases of heatstroke) and one particularly sad death. Five-year-old Edward Clark died when he fell three stories from the roof of his home while watching the event.

Throughout the rest of the year, Newark Airport appeared in the little social fillers announcing the comings and goings of local residents, hinting at the use that the place was getting. G.A. Bradshaw had a regular column in the *Trenton Evening Times* highlighting some feature of the Garden State with an illustration. The October 2, 1941 installment, "Know New Jersey—No. 39," was Newark Airport, quoting from state government promotion: "Through an elaborate and practical air traffic control system at this recently reopened spacious and well-equipped airport, commercial, private and military aircraft are directed and accommodated without delay."

News from Newark had made newspapers across the country before—often bad news. But now the headlines were something to be proud of. On October 5, the *Dallas Morning News* featured a photo of a new long-range dive bomber being produced by Brewster and billed as a "Super-Stuka," referencing the German Stukas raining terror down on Europe. This was the same model SB 2A-1 that slid into a landing from failed landing gear the month before, but the photo showed a more successful test flight with William S. Knudsen at the stick. It was a triumphant image, one full of bravado that this plane—this *American* plane—was better than the similar plane the Germans had.

But the war was closing in.

Individually, Americans were joining foreign forces or looking to assist the Allies where they could. Joseph Price, a twenty-nine-year-old from White Plains, New York, was among them. Originally from England, he had become an American citizen and worked at the Brewster Aeronautical Corporation plant at Newark Airport. Seeing his homeland in peril, he left his job and was sailing for England with other American civilian technicians. On November 6, 1941, he was listed among the seventeen dead—including three New Jerseyans—when a German U-boat sunk their ship.

Fog—even thick enough to shut down an airport—is nothing unusual. And yet, in retrospect, knowing what was coming, it is possible to read some melodramatic symbolism into the thick curtain of it that was drawn across Newark Airport three minutes to midnight on December 3—dogging an American Air Lines plane that landed just before the field was closed.

Three days later, the Japanese would attack Pearl Harbor.

WORLD WAR II

Patrons to Charles Flynn's West Orange, New Jersey tavern sought to escape the bad news of war by tossing back a beer or two and pumping nickels into the jukebox. Among their favorite tunes was "Jersey Bounce," written by Tiny Bradshaw, Eddie Johnson and Bobby Plater with lyrics by Buddy Feyne (under the name Robert B. Wright to avoid conflicts with an ASCAP strike). It hit number one in 1942 as an instrumental, covered by Benny Goodman. Several other versions would be recorded over the years, including those by Jimmy Dorsey, Glenn Miller and Ella Fitzgerald. It was so popular that "Jersey Bounce" was painted on the nose art of many a bomber.

But as patrons at Flynn's Tavern tried to swing—or bounce—to the music, they found their fun interrupted by the latest weather report that somehow got stuck into the middle of the music. It seemed to be coming from an airport, and with a war on and a worry over spies, this interception caught the attention of the FBI. So agents paid Flynn's a visit and pumped nickel after nickel into the machine and heard a weather report interrupting pretty much every song. In one of the stranger Garden State war stories, it was believed somehow that the jukebox electronics unintentionally picked up weather reports from Newark Airport!

While it had a military presence almost since it opened and, to some degree, the war mobilization helped to revive it, the reality of U.S. involvement in the war gave Newark Airport a larger role in building up American airpower. Control over operations was handed over to the Army Air Corps in 1942. Civilian air travel was curtailed to reserve resources for the military, and Newark was the home of ramped-up aviation manufacturing and some of the army's pilot training—it was even home base to a USO unit.

On May 16, 1944, Newark Airport was the scene of the first and largest in-country medical evacuation of the war. Two hundred men and three women, wounded overseas badly enough for a ticket stateside, were loaded onto a dozen of the army's new C-47 ambulance aircraft. They were headed for hospitals in Indianapolis, Boston, Cleveland and Battle Creek, Michigan. But it wouldn't be the last such evacuation. Repeat performances were expected that following Wednesday and Thursday.

New Jerseyans stressed by the long war, however, found warmhearted relief in January 1945, when an army plane landed at Newark with an unexpected package—a little dog that had hitchhiked via airplane some 13,512 miles from New Guinea to New Jersey. The pooch had arrived on the West Coast and been sent to Newark by way of Memphis, Tennessee, and Greensboro, North Carolina. The express shipment tag around his neck read he was on his way to "My Mistress: Marilyn Diana Schwartz" of Jersey City, adding, "Don't Stop Me Now…" The little dog seemed to take right away to his new owner, the two-year-old Ms. Schwartz, who promptly—and perhaps ironically, given his mode of transport—named him "Choo-Choo," in honor of his voyaging ways. The identity of the sender was officially a mystery, but Schwartz's mother, Rose, confided to reporters it was likely her cousin, Pfc. Mortimer Miller, who was last heard from serving in New Guinea. The pup brightened not only young Ms. Schwartz's day but also the days of the army men tending him at the different legs of his journey, who tallied up the miles he had traveled on his express tag when he reached them. It was just the kind of sweet story a war-weary nation needed, and pictures of Choo-Choo in little Marilyn's arms appeared in newspapers around the country.

But Newark Airport played a role that didn't make headlines during the war. Throughout the conflict, captured enemy technology was returned to the United States for study. After the fall of Berlin, without Nazi resistance, however, it was possible to send teams to search Germany's research facilities, seizing scientific reports and weapons. Perhaps the most significant windfall was from Operation Paperclip, which brought rocket technology—and rocket scientists, like Wernher von Braun—over to America, laying the foundations of the United States space program. Less well known was Project Lusty—an adolescent-sounding stretch of an acronym derived from "LUftwaffe Secret TechnologY." Launched by the Army Air Force's Exploitation Division, it was to seize and return to the United States examples of German aircraft technology—including jet aircraft. Operation Lusty was carried out by two teams, one tasked with grabbing physical aircraft and weapons and the other with securing documents.

The first team was headed by Colonel Harold E. Watson, a test pilot, who recruited other pilots, aviation engineers and maintenance crews into what became known as "Watson's Whizzers." After V-E Day, the Whizzers even picked up Luftwaffe and German test pilots—giving them the choice of a prison camp or flying with them. Given a "Black List" of desired aircraft, the Whizzers traveled throughout Europe, ironically mostly by jeep, hunting them down and securing examples. Once they had them, however, they had to be transported back to the United States. Under the Lend-Lease program, the United States gave the British navy an escort carrier, the USS *Winjah*, which they promptly rechristened with the tougher sounding name RMS *Reaper*. The Brits were willing to lend the ship back for use in transporting the captured aircraft the Whizzers flew to a port at Cherbourg, France.

They were offloaded at Port Newark and sent over to Newark Airport, where they were studied and sent on to other bases at Freeman Field in Indiana or the Naval Air Station Patuxent River in Maryland.

After the war, on August 1, 1947, the Army Air Force celebrated its fortieth anniversary with a massive flight of over one hundred aircraft over New Jersey as part of the ceremonies at Newark Airport. The specific branch existed only since June 1941 but was a direct descendant of the Aeronautical Division of the Signal Corps—the first heavier-than-air military force, founded August 1, 1907. On September 26, 1947, the United States Air Force would officially be spun off as its own, independent branch.

PORT AUTHORITY

By the middle of 1946, the idea was floated that Newark Airport should be bought from the City of Newark by the Port of New York Authority.

Despite the Empire State featuring in the name (it would later be changed to the Port Authority of New York and New Jersey), this was a bi-state agency established in 1921 to operate the commercial infrastructures of both New York and New Jersey—interstate highways, tunnels, rails and seaports. The idea of adding airports to the Port Authority made sense. It became a plank in the platform of New Jersey's Democrats as they geared up for the coming gubernatorial campaign. Taking the airport off Newark's hands was part of a larger plan that also included buying LaGuardia Airport and Idlewild Airport (later renamed John F. Kennedy International Airport), as well as Newark's seaport, the Hudson and Manhattan Railroad and some forty thousand acres of Newark Bay marshlands for future reclamation and development.

The notion was bipartisan enough that New Jersey's incumbent governor, the Republican Walter Evans Edge, met with the Port Authority's representatives to discuss just how viable it really was. In order to fit into the overall vision of growth, however, Newark Airport would need to be expanded and upgraded. By August 1946, the Port Authority submitted a $76 million, forty-three-page proposal to the Newark City commissioners for the air and seaports, to be paid for by issuing thirty-year bonds. It would triple Newark Airport's capacity, expanding the property across the border from Essex County into Union, making it necessary to offer Newark (in Essex) $100,000 a year and Elizabeth (in Union) $16,000 a year, in lieu of taxes. Creating a greater system of airports, Port Authority commissioner Bayard F. Pope argued, was critical for the region. "If we cannot handle this air traffic," Pope told reporters, "it will seek the terminal facilities in other sections of the east."

Supporters of this plan saw it as a win for New Jersey as a whole but particularly for the city of Newark, which had been running the airport at a deficit for years. Indeed, it was this lack of cash that many argued was holding it back from becoming a world-class terminal. "The financial inability of Newark to continue the maintenance and operation of Newark Airport in a manner required by the phenomenal growth of commercial aviation during the last few years has long been apparent," stated an editorial in the *Trenton Evening Times*. Annual deficits had run as much as $415,000, risking "making the city's great investment in the enterprise…virtually a total loss."

Some in Newark, however, didn't see it that way.

The city commissioners held out, and the next month, the Port Authority upped the total cash payments over thirty years to Newark from $750,000,000 to $900,202,500. There was likely a little bit of bruised pride here. The head of the commission was none other than ex-mayor Meyer C. Ellenstein, who had fought the running battles with LaGuardia and was always very possessive of the airport—even when money was put up to turn it into an independent nonprofit corporation. He released a twenty-five-page statement outlining his opposition to the leasing of the airport. He was, perhaps tellingly, fine with leasing the seaport. But when it came to the airport, he counseled that the city "mark time" and wait for the federal government to come around to the idea that aviation was really their province. Other critics of the total plan saw it as the Port Authority operating for profit rather than servicing bonds and operating expenses.

Despite deadlock on the city commission, the momentum was definitely in favor of the plan. New Jersey, after all, had been investing heavily in improving the highways around Newark's airport and seaports, establishing the beefed-up infrastructure needed to support the vision many held for the future. By April 1947, then-governor Alfred Driscoll signed off on three bills that had passed the legislature, clearing the way, as far as the state was concerned, for negotiations for the Port Authority's acquisitions. By July 10,

Newark Airport was just one component of a larger transportation nexus that converged on Newark, New Jersey. *Courtesy of the Newark Public Library.*

it had cleared another hurdle when Newark's mayor, Vincent J. Murphy, announced the legal paperwork had been taken care of. Informal word had it that the Port Authority was ready to formally agree to the city's proposal to receive a full 75 percent of the profits from the seaport and airport.

Then, at last, on October 23, 1947, the Port Authority of New York officially took over Newark Airport in a fifty-year lease. It just about squeaked by the Newark City Commission by a three-to-two vote. But with it, the Port Authority would bring $55 million to spend on improvements. Along with LaGuardia and Idlewild, it created the largest airport operating entity in the world. The *Trenton Evening Times*, which had supported the deal all along, said in an editorial that, given how the airport was something of a burden to Newark, which was holding back the facility's long-term growth, "[i]t is hard to see why opposition to the lease has been so determined and so long."

Perhaps it was the ghost of Newark's ex-mayor, Thomas Raymond, that stoked the opposition. Certainly some could still remember when having a world-class airport was a source of pride for the city, in days before its glory was stolen by New York. But by the approach of mid-century, the aviation industry had grown more vast than even the ambitions and egos of either city or either state.

The Garden and the Empire States would need to learn to work together.

TRAGEDY

Of course, Newark Airport's history wasn't without its tragic accidents. Aircraft that had taken off from or were heading to the airport sometimes disappeared, crashing somewhere along the way. But two little-remembered accidents surprisingly resonate with us today. We think of hijacking and terrorism on the wing as an ill of our age. Yet, on October 10, 1933, a United Air Lines flight, hopscotching its way from Newark Airport to Oakland, California, was believed to have been brought down in the first proven act of sabotage in the history of commercial aviation. The Boeing 247 Propliner had landed at Cleveland and just taken off for its next stop in Chicago when it exploded en route, raining debris down near Chesterton, Indiana, shortly after 9:00 p.m. The four passengers and three crew members were killed. The evidence pointed to an explosion in the baggage compartment. The fuel tanks were crushed in, for example, meaning they had not exploded. Clues led investigators to believe the explosion was caused by a nitroglycerin device, but no suspect was ever identified and the case remains unsolved to this day.

When terrorists flew two hijacked passenger airliners into the Twin Towers on September 11, 2001, it put some old enough to remember in mind of another time when an aircraft slammed into a famous building. On July 28, 1945, a B-25 bomber, lost in the foggy night, crashed into the 102nd floor of the Empire State Building. Given that this event involved the world's tallest building at the time—an icon of the New York skyline—it has retained a place in the history books. But on May 20, 1946—just ten months afterward—another airplane struck a building in the heart of the financial district on an equally fog-ridden night. A twin-engine army C-45 from Smyrna, Tennessee, was on its way to Newark Airport. At a time when pilots placed greater reliance on visual clues to navigate than they do today, it was speculated the pilot was looking for the Hudson River as his cue to turn off toward the approach to Newark. He may have actually been over the East River, however, and his banking maneuver took him straight into the 58th floor of 40 Wall Street, the 71-story Bank of Manhattan Company Building. All five passengers were killed.

LIBERTY

While Newark Airport's fortunes ebbed and flowed with those of the industry that it helped to establish, the second half of the twentieth century saw expansion and renovation. The original administration building, with

The North Terminal as it appeared in the early 1960s. *Courtesy of Joseph Bond.*

its first air traffic control tower, was retired in 1953, replaced with the larger North Terminal.

Ray Shapp, a pilot for United Air Lines for some thirty-two years and a flight instructor (now retired), relates how Newark's North Terminal had something of a reputation. "One of my pilot friends was a good ole southern boy," he says. "In reference to the wretched conditions of the passenger facilities, he said passengers traveling through [Newark's airport] were in more need of the sick sack in the terminal than in the worst turbulence aloft. At United, a long narrow finger pier jutted out from the main terminal building. Except for the places where the airlines posted their logo, the decor was sickly yellow on faded and mottled gray. Passengers exited through gates at ground level exposed to the weather and boarded their flights via movable stairs or stairs that were extended from inside their aircraft."

The North Terminal has since been demolished—perhaps for the better—but the original administration building was listed on the National Register of Historic Places in 1979. As with so many historic but outmoded buildings, however, it sat neglected for years. It was given a second life in 2004 when it was moved and refurbished as the airport's offices.

In the 1970s, the North Terminal was torn down and replaced over time with the three buildings we now know. Change also came to the structure of running the place. The Port Authority still runs Terminal B, but Terminal

John McKeon, a Port Authority engineer, surveys the progress on building the new terminals at Newark Airport in 1970. The project cost over $200 million. *Courtesy of the Newark Public Library.*

The new terminals from the air. *Courtesy of the Newark Public Library.*

A has been operated by United Airlines and Terminal C by Continental Airlines. With the merger of United and Continental, Newark will be their third largest hub in the country.

One change in particular, however, was particularly painful to come by. Accidents, while less common than they used to be, have remained part of aviation life. But those experienced by planes in or out of Newark had been just that—*accidents*, caused by mechanical failure or human error. On September 11, 2001, Americans were stunned to see hijacked airplanes used as weapons, being intentionally flown into buildings. United Airlines Flight 93 took off from Newark on that clear, crisp morning, heading for San Francisco. Shortly after takeoff, it was commandeered by terrorists, as were three other passenger planes. Two were flown into each of the Twin Towers of Manhattan's World Trade Center, while a third crashed into the Pentagon just outside Washington, D.C., in Virginia. Realizing what was happening, passengers onboard Flight 93 attempted to overpower the hijackers, but the plane plunged into a field in Shanksville, Pennsylvania, killing all onboard.

It is believed that it was intended to be crashed into the White House or Capitol in Washington, D.C.

"Flight 93 was under the command of Captain Jason Dahl who was a Standards Captain assigned to United's Training Center in Denver," retired United pilot Ray Shapp notes. "Standards Captains are expected to 'displace' a regular line captain at least once every 90 days in order to remain current with actual line operations. If he hadn't voluntarily arranged to have flight 93 assigned to him, the regular captain (probably a local resident) would have flown that trip. The copilot, LeRoy Homer, was from Marlton, New Jersey."

The next year, in a gesture to those who died that terrible day, the word "Liberty" was inserted into the name, making it Newark Liberty International Airport.

The industry of flying has become both better and, perhaps, worse. Flying is significantly safer yet also more expensive and, at times, something of a hassle with long lines, cramped seats and security restrictions. Still, for all the inconveniences, the remarkable act of flight has become, equally remarkably, commonplace. What would Thomas Raymond or Meyer Ellenstein think if they could know that in 2010, Newark's airport had 403,880 aircraft operations serving 33,107,041 travelers, making it the tenth busiest in the nation?

So if you find yourself standing in line at Newark Airport, or waiting to pick up someone whose flight was delayed, perhaps pass some of the time remembering the long and rich history all around you. It might not make the line move any faster, but maybe it will help you to better appreciate the marvel it represents.

CHAPTER 7

"To Cast a Freedman's Vote"

How a Handyman from Perth Amboy Made Civil Rights History

The night Barack Obama gave his acceptance speech following his election as the forty-fourth president of the United States, among those who paused to listen to the president-elect were those old enough to remember a time when men and women who looked like him couldn't drink from the same water fountain or eat at the same lunch counter. In the audience were people who marched on places like Selma and Birmingham. Commentators evoked the names of martyrs to the cause, like Dr. Martin Luther King Jr. and Malcolm X. Others still called up the less distinct memory of the masses of humanity who had toiled their lives away as slaves.

The historic nature of that election rises above the partisanship of politics, regardless of one's political persuasion or opinions of his administration. But while his achieving the highest office in the land might be a high-water mark in the civil rights movement, it was, ultimately, just the latest chapter in a long and ongoing story of how humans in America deal with race. Still, it did provide an organic moment to pause and consider the journey thus far.

The face that came to my mind that night was that of a handyman from Perth Amboy, New Jersey, who cast the first African American ballot under the auspices of the Fifteenth Amendment to the U.S. Constitution in 1870.

THE FIFTEENTH AMENDMENT

Do a Google search on "Thomas Mundy Peterson" and it is his historic vote that comes up again and again but scant little else. While that bit of trivia may be important, the real interest lies in the convergence of all that had to come together to make that moment possible—and everything that came after. And, of course, Peterson was more than an event. Who was he as a man? How did that moment change his life?

Obviously, in order to become the first voter under the Fifteenth Amendment, there had to be a Fifteenth Amendment in the first place.

Slavery had been part of New Jersey history right from the very beginnings. When Lords John Berkely and George Carteret were enticing settlers to their new property, they promised an extra seventy-five acres for every slave someone brought along. The wharves of Perth Amboy saw ships direct from Africa unloading human cargo, shuffled off in clanking chains to barracks on the corner of Smith and Water Streets, awaiting sale in the town square—in front of the same city hall where Peterson would eventually cast his vote.

The issue of slavery has been likened to a sleeping snake, metaphorically coiled under the table, as the founders fussed and fought over the Constitution that would define the nation they were creating. Unresolved for various reasons, it would, in less than a century, indeed come back to bite the country.

Westward expansion at last brought the question to a head—would these new territories be brought into the Republic as slave states or free? Reaching critical mass, the struggle to answer those questions exploded in the four-year spasm of violence that we call the American Civil War.

President Abraham Lincoln is often referred to as the man who freed the slaves. This laudable title usually refers to his Emancipation Proclamation—his executive order of January 1, 1863. In truth, this was more of a declaration of intent. For one thing, it only applied to the ten states in rebellion. While it nevertheless translated into freedom for slaves found in Rebel territory taken by Union soldiers, it did not specifically outlaw slavery in the nation as a whole.

A true transitioning away from slavery, however, would require more work even after the Union's victory. In considering the Fifteenth Amendment, one must take it in context with the Thirteenth and Fourteenth, a three-piece set known as the Restoration Amendments.

Considering the bloody war that gave it birth, the Thirteenth Amendment to the U.S. Constitution seems rather stark, with a straightforward simplicity of language: "Neither slavery nor involuntary servitude, except as a punishment for crime whereof the party shall have been duly convicted, shall exist within the United States, or any place subject to their jurisdiction."

That's all it took—in theory anyway—to set into motion the once-and-for-all end of slavery in the United States. Of course, that bit of paperwork wasn't going to change the ingrained racial attitudes of those who had just defended that "peculiar institution." And what did it really mean to those it claimed to release from bondage? What did it mean to be "free"? What was the legal status of the millions of men, women and children those words affected? Were they citizens, with all the rights and responsibilities that status conferred?

The Fourteenth Amendment, passed in 1868, was intended to answer those questions and is perhaps necessarily a longer text, consisting of five sections, mostly dealing with how to proportion representation after this overnight surge in citizens. But the first section is what was pertinent to all those now–ex slaves:

> *All persons born or naturalized in the United States, and subject to the jurisdiction thereof, are citizens of the United States and of the State wherein they reside. No State shall make or enforce any law which shall abridge the privileges or immunities of citizens of the United States; nor shall any State deprive any person of life, liberty, or property, without due process of law; nor deny to any person within its jurisdiction the equal protection of the laws.*

Individual colonies and states had long ago established bans on importing slaves from outside nations—not out of any desire to curb the institution as much as protect the interests of slave traders at home. So by 1868, pretty much all the people freed by the Thirteenth Amendment had been born here. With one broad, inclusive stroke, the Fourteenth Amendment conferred citizenship on the entirety of that population. The Fourteenth Amendment was a direct repudiation of the 1857 *Dred Scott v. Sanford* Supreme Court decision that established that Negros were not citizens.

Resistance, of course, would be inevitable. People who held tight enough to principles—racist though they may be—to actually fight, kill and die for them, were hardly going to be swayed by laws passed by a government most viewed as illegitimate occupiers. A range of tactics were employed by those seeking to prevent Negro inclusion in civil society—from the outright brutal intimidation of the Ku Klux Klan to the restrictive legislative loopholes of the so-called Jim Crow laws. State constitutions still asserted the right to limit suffrage based on race or on having been a slave—or even having been the child or grandchild of a slave.

Race, however, wasn't the only issue. Women would be denied the right to vote regardless of race or other status for another fifty years. Even acceptance of Jesus Christ as your Lord and Savior was a criterion for a handful of states—the establishment clause of the First Amendment notwithstanding. And when race *was* the central issue, it wasn't always specifically about dark skin—some wanted the recent influx of Irish and Chinese immigrants kept out of voting too. Of course, the tools of exclusion worked both ways. Southern Republicans had been using loyalty oaths to stem the influence of ex-Confederates.

Nevertheless, by March 30, 1870, enough states had ratified the Fifteenth Amendment to make it the law in another remarkably straightforward piece of language: "The right of citizens of the United States to vote shall not be denied or abridged by the United States or by any State on account of race, color, or previous condition of servitude."

It isn't known how closely Thomas Peterson had been following the debates that preceded ratification. But certainly others in Perth Amboy were watching.

EAGLESWOOD

John Lawrence Kearny. *Courtesy of John Kerry Dyke.*

"I was working for Mr. J.L. Kearny on the morning of the day of the election, and did not think of voting until he came out to the stable where I was attending to the horses and advised me to go to the polls and exercise a citizen's privilege," Thomas Peterson later told a reporter. The question of the day was whether the city of Perth Amboy should revise its existing charter or abandon it to return to a previous township form of government. "When I went home to dinner at noon I met Mr. Marcus Spring of Eagleswood, a place about a mile out of town, and he, too, advised me to claim the right of suffrage at the polls."

It probably wasn't mere coincidence that Marcus Spring (1810–1874) was there to encourage Peterson to go vote. In 1853, with his wife, Rebecca (1812–1911), he established the Raritan Bay

Union, a sort of progressive cross between a boarding school, artist colony and utopian community. Not only did male and female students share the classroom, but black and white did, as well as other races. Girls were encouraged to do things like public speaking, to engage in sports and perform plays—things any respectable young lady would never be taught in most schools of the day. The Raritan Bay Union attracted an impressive array of progressive liberals, artists and reformers to Perth Amboy. Angelina and Sarah Grimké (the abolitionist and women's suffrage activist sisters) taught classes while Angelina's husband, Theodore Weld (considered the father of modern American abolitionism), ran the school. Among those who lived or worked at the Raritan Bay Union were the influential author Caroline Kirkland; Kentucky-born abolitionist, politician and jurist James Birney; American landscape painter George Inness; portrait artist William Page; social reformist Edward Palmer; teacher, writer, philosopher and reformer Amos Bronson Alcott; and Henry David Thoreau. Thoreau enjoyed surveying land and indulged his interest by surveying Eagleswood's 260 acres.

But to get a real sense of the Springs and the strength of the ideals that underlay their vision, one needs to look at Rebecca Spring's reaction to John Brown's famous raid on Harpers

Marcus Spring, circa 1870. *Courtesy of John Kerry Dyke.*

Rebecca Spring. *Courtesy of John Kerry Dyke.*

Ferry. Between October 16 and 19, 1859, the white abolitionist John Brown attempted to incite a slave uprising by leading a group of sixteen white men, three free blacks, one freed slave and one fugitive slave to seize the U.S. arsenal at Harpers Ferry, Virginia. They were defeated by U.S. Marines and militia, under the perhaps now prescient command of Robert E. Lee. When the smoke cleared, ten of Brown's men were dead. Four managed to escape but were later captured. Seven were seized immediately, including Brown himself. All would be hanged.

Rebecca Spring came to Brown's Charlestown, Virginia jail cell and tended to his wounds. She also administered to Aaron Stevens and Absolom Hazlett. The bodies of some of the executed men would be claimed and brought home. Two apparently ended up as teaching cadavers at medical schools. But when no one claimed the bodies of Stevens and Hazlett, she was determined that they would be buried in *free* soil. She would bring them back to Perth Amboy to graves on the Springs' Eagleswood estate. That was a strong abolitionist statement. But the men were also convicted of treason, and when Perth Amboy's citizens got wind of Rebecca Spring's intentions, they were outraged. So the bodies of the two men were landed instead at Rahway and, under the cover of darkness, brought to Eagleswood, where they would remain until 1899, when they were transferred to a cemetery at North Elba, New York.

John Brown's two now-fatherless daughters would find an education with Theodore Weld at the Raritan Bay Union. It is little wonder that Eagleswood became a stop on the Underground Railroad.

The Raritan Bay Union disbanded in 1860 but was replaced by the Springs with the Eagleswood Military Academy. It tried to carry on the same kind of progressivism, but perhaps with some irony, the Civil War ended the

A contemporary drawing of the Eagleswood Academy. The progressive attitudes of its graduates seem to have influenced how Perth Amboy reacted to Peterson's vote. *Courtesy of John Kerry Dyke.*

experiment. Many of the teachers and students went off to serve, leaving a less economically viable institution behind them.

By the war's end, their school no longer existed, but the Springs were still committed to the ideals it had taught. Indeed, there was a generation of Perth Amboy's leading citizens who had graduated, infused with such ideals—including James Lawrence Kearny.

It was dumb luck that the first post-ratification election in which any black person could vote happened to be in Perth Amboy. But now there was a Fifteenth Amendment and a community influenced by a zeal to see Negro suffrage become reality. All that was needed was a black man to step up to meet that destiny.

SLAVE OR FREE?

When Thomas Peterson came into this world on October 6, 1824, deep within his cells, somewhere between just four and six genes determined what the rest of his life would probably be like. They regulated the amount and type of something called melanin—a pigment that would shade his skin. His DNA, handed down through his African ancestors, gave him other distinctive physical traits—the color and texture of his hair, the shape of his nose and lips. In the eyes of much of the society into which he was born, such features marked one as an inferior creature. Inferior enough, in fact, that for over 7,500 men and women in New Jersey alone, it justified their being held in involuntary bondage and servitude.

Relatively speaking, Peterson was lucky. A "gradual emancipation" law had been passed in New Jersey twenty years before he was born. It didn't help those already held as slaves, but it meant that, since he was born afterward, he would never have to personally know what it meant to be the property of another. But that reality was only as far away as his parents and in the lingering attitudes of some of his white neighbors.

The story of Peterson's childhood is sketchy at best, though not for want of trying by local historians. He was born in what is now Metuchen (then part of Woodbridge), and local historians Tyreen Reuter and Walter Stochel have been researching that part of his life. His parents were Thomas and Lucy, and their story is something of a muddle if you go by the various subsequent articles and histories that mention them. When Thomas Peterson died in 1904, the *Newark Evening News* described his parents as having both been slaves owned by the same Mundy family. This was repeated in a 1959 *Perth Amboy Evening News* article. In his *History of Perth Amboy*, William C. McGinnis says the elder Thomas was "employed" by the Mundys, while Lucy's parents were slaves of Monmouth County's Newell family. A 1977 *Perth Amboy Evening News* article, however, says Thomas Sr. was born to free parents while Lucy was born to slaves.

Why the ambiguity?

Well, at least in the instances of newspapers, it can likely be put down to harried reporters looking to make a deadline and not having time to check facts too deeply. But there is also something alluringly melodramatic in the image of the son of slaves casting that first vote as a free man. The reality is a little more complicated.

We do know that Thomas Sr. was indeed associated with the Mundys, an old Metuchen family dating back to 1665, when Nicholas Mundy came over from England and called the place home. The specific member of the family who evidently owned or employed Thomas Sr. was Ezra Mundy (1772–1841). Whether it was an owner-slave or employer-employee relationship isn't yet entirely clear. It is certainly possible it could have been both—that Thomas was a slave but manumitted and stayed on as paid labor.

Lucy is a little easier to follow. She had been a slave of Hugh Newell (1744–1816) of Freehold Township. Some historians go out of their way to point out that this is the same Newell family that had also produced William Augustus Newell (1817–901)—New Jersey's delegate to the U.S. House of Representatives (1847–1851 and again 1865–1867), state governor (1857–1860), governor of the Washington Territory (now Washington State, 1880–1884) and author of the Newell Act that created the United States Life-Saving Service (a precursor to the United States Coast Guard).

Hugh Newell, however, is the one that's important to our story. He settled in Freehold Township from Ireland and saw service in the War for Independence. Evidently, he had other servants, as he is found in 1767 advertising a reward in the *Pennsylvania Gazette* for the return of an Irish servant by the name of John M'Cullough. Newell died in 1816, but on April 24, 1822, his executors officially manumitted the twenty-two-year-old Lucy.

How Lucy—who is sometimes identified as Lucy Green—found her way from Freehold in Monmouth County to Woodbridge in Middlesex County isn't entirely clear, but she obviously did as she is found marrying Thomas Sr. on January 27, 1820. The event was included in a list of marriages performed by Reverend Henry Cook in the records of the Second Presbyterian Church of Woodbridge (now the First Presbyterian Church of Metuchen) and offers a clue as to how she might have gotten to Woodbridge.

The list records the marriage between "Thomas, a black man of Ezra Mundy," and "Lucy, a black woman of John Smock." What's striking is that the marriage took place two years *before* Lucy was freed, yet she is identified as being "of John Smock."

Assuming we're talking about the same Thomas and Lucy—and there isn't any reason to believe we're not—we can make some reasonable speculations. It wasn't unusual for slaves to be "lent" to others, who would be responsible for them, though legal ownership remained technically with the original master. It is plausible that when Newell died, the family didn't need her and so sent her off to someone who did—either a friend, relative or someone who paid them for her services. The relationship between the Newells and Smock is still being explored.

If Lucy was twenty-two in 1822 when she was freed, she was born around 1800—too early to fall under the 1804 Gradual Emancipation Act in New Jersey. So she was, as far as the law was concerned, a slave until the Newells emancipated her. Nevertheless, there may have been an arrangement that she would be freed after age twenty-one—the age girls born to slave mothers were to be freed under the act. While the exact circumstances are not known, Lucy may have understood that she would not need to return to Monmouth County and so could marry and set down roots in Middlesex County.

In any event, four years after they were married, Thomas Jr. came into the world—the son of a free mother.

According to McGinnis—who takes much of his information from contemporary newspaper articles—the family moved to Perth Amboy in 1828, and Thomas Sr. died shortly thereafter. We can say he was alive at least in 1830, as well as get an idea of what the family consisted of, thanks to the 1830 U.S. Census. Back then, the censuses were little more than general headcounts, with individuals grouped by the broad categories of sex, race and age bracket. Nevertheless, even these limited data points can be mined for clues.

Thomas Sr. gave his name as Thomas Mundy. That makes sense given his association with the Mundy family. But last names are fluid and indistinct quantities in this story. McGinnis says the elder Thomas was a Peterson. If this is correct, why did he identify himself to the census-taker as Mundy? His son, Thomas, appears over the years as both Thomas Peterson and Thomas Mundy. Exactly when and with whom the Peterson name came into play isn't clear. A literal interpretation might be that Thomas Sr. was the son of someone named Peter. Peterson seems to have been the "real" family name, but they evidently had no objections to also being known as Mundy—a fact that is suggestive.

There is reason to think that the relationship between the white Mundys and their black servants was, relatively speaking, a positive one. Census records show a free African American family with the last name of Mundy living in the same neighborhood as the Caucasian families of the same name. If someone treats you badly, you probably won't adopt their last name and live next to them if you can help it.

The makeup of Thomas and Lucy's family can be hinted at by the 1830 census, showing them living in Perth Amboy. The elder Thomas is represented by the single free Negro male in the category of age thirty-six to fifty-five. That would make his birth somewhere between 1775 and 1795. Lucy would be the single free Negro woman in the age-twenty-four-to-thirty-six bracket. We know she was born around 1800, so she would be thirty years old, making her husband at least six years her senior.

Thomas Jr. would be one of the three boys in the under-ten-years-old category, and there was a girl in the ten-to-twenty-four category. We have to be a little careful here—these headcount censuses don't list the relationship of the counted to the head of the household. Later censuses would add this information, but it can't be said with complete certainty that these were all representative of parents and their children. Nevertheless, it seems at least reasonable to assume that by 1830, Thomas Jr. had two brothers and a big sister.

While the idea of anyone "owning" another human being is repugnant to modern sensibilities, human relationships are often far more complicated than that odious state might imply. Regardless of what Thomas Sr. was to Ezra Mundy—slave, servant, employee—there is another clue that their relationship held at least some warmth. We know of this thanks to a matter-of-fact statement in a newspaper article talking about Thomas Peterson found by Walter Stochel. It is undated but has to at least post-date 1884 and pre-date Peterson's death in 1904. "'Tom' is a well educated negro," it reads, in the paternalistic language typical of the time. "When a young man he was bound out to Izra Mundy, NJ of Metuchen, by whose name he has been called." They misspelled Ezra's name as "Izra" and misidentified his birth year as 1829, so who knows how trustworthy the information really is. But, if it is true, Thomas Sr. wouldn't indenture out his son to the man if he himself had been mistreated by him.

The 1804 Gradual Emancipation Act began New Jersey's slow withdrawal from the slavery paradigm, though not necessarily from the deeply rooted racial attitudes that had made it possible. The act set the somewhat arbitrary date of July 4, 1804, as the cutoff—if you were a black person fortunate enough to have been born on July 5, 1804, you were considered free, even if your mother remained a slave. If you were born July 3, 1804, tough luck. Anyone born prior to the date was considered an "apprentice for life." A slave by any other name…

Those born afterward to slave parents were required to serve a more limited apprenticeship in the service of whoever owned their mother. On the one hand, there was some logic to it—presumably, they would be brought up in some trade or with some skills that would enable them to earn their way in life as adults, akin to a vocational education. But, in practice, it was as much a way of extending their servitude just that much longer. Girls would be free at age twenty-one and boys at age twenty-five. Since Thomas Jr. was born to Lucy after her manumission, it is presumed that the apprenticeship with Ezra was a mutually voluntary arrangement.

DAPHNE

The act required some paperwork. Records needed to be made of all births to enslaved mothers after July 4, 1804. So, on April 18, 1823, Andrew Bell of Perth Amboy dutifully filed, "I do hereby certify that a Negro woman named Bett, [sic] a Slave belonging to me was delivered of a female child named Daphne on the eighth day of October, 1820."

Daphne would grow up to marry Thomas Jr. on February 10, 1844—and her association with the Bell family would prove important to their future.

Andrew Bell is an interesting character in his own right. He was born on June 4, 1757, in Philadelphia, but the family soon moved to New Jersey. He studied law under Cortlandt Skinner in Perth Amboy, where Bell's father, a British army officer, had built a fine house. Andrew remained a Loyalist during the American Revolution. He joined the British army, serving as a clerk for the British command in New York, including under Sir Henry Clinton. But it wasn't all quill-pushing—he saw action in several skirmishes and the Battle of Monmouth. His diary of his time in service remains a valuable resource for historians.

One might assume that a Loyalist staunch enough to take up arms in the cause would have been forced to hightail it out of Perth Amboy when the British lost the war, as so many of his fellow Loyalists did. Yet while the house he inherited from his father in 1778 was confiscated the following year, Andrew Bell remained in New Jersey the rest of his life.

That he was able to remain unmolested was likely due to a fortuitous family connection through marriage. In 1779, his sister, Cornelia (1755–1783), had married William Paterson, who most certainly came down quite firmly on the side opposite that of his new brother-in-law. Where other men of his generation chased glory on the battlefield, Paterson found his arena of service in the perhaps more mundane, but equally crucial, task of helping to create a working system of government for an America that would—hopefully—soon need one. He represented Somerset County in the provincial assembly and was its secretary when it signed the new constitution that established it as a state—and in a state of rebellion against Great Britain. As New Jersey's first attorney general, he somehow managed to keep some semblance of law and order amidst the chaos of war. When it came time to consider a national government, Paterson represented New Jersey at the Constitutional Conventions, where he offered the so-called New Jersey Plan in the debates over how the legislature would be structured and representation determined. Paterson went on to become New Jersey's first senator (1789–1790) and second governor (1790–1793).

A powerful and influential man, indeed, for ex-Loyalist Andrew Bell to have for a brother-in-law. He was able to settle back into his Perth Amboy estate and start life over as a successful merchant with his wife, Susanna. Whatever hard feelings there might have been over the war, they were brushed aside enough by 1806 for him to be appointed as surveyor general for the East Jersey Proprietors—a position he would hold until 1842. He remained active with St. Peter's Episcopal Church, serving as a churchwarden. In 1787, his name appears on a petition to the New Jersey Legislative Council seeking permission to hold a lottery to help rebuild the church. In the church's archives, I came across Bell's handwritten recipe for producing industrial-sized quantities of ginger wine.

When Andrew Bell sat down to write his will, he and Susanna had no children to leave anything to, but he was not without other family, friends and causes to name as beneficiaries. St. Peter's, for example, received a $300 trust to fund needed repairs to the church and rectory. He left another trust of $400 to be used to help Perth Amboy's poor, to be administered by another William Paterson, his great-nephew (the William Paterson who married Bell's sister died in 1806).

But he also remembered Daphne and her sister, Jane, who had been their servants, both born of their slave, Betty. According to his will:

> *I give and Bequeath to my said wife my coloured female servant Jane until she arrives at the age of twenty one years* [the age at which girls were

released from their "apprenticeships"] *at which period I Give and Bequeath to my Executors the sum of Five Hundred Dollars in trust for her benefit, and I also Give and Bequeath to my said Executors the like sum of Five Hundred Dollars in trust for the benefit of my female servant Daphne who has lately arrived at the age of twenty one years and I direct my said Executors to deposit the said two sums of Five Hundred Dollars each in the Savings Bank of New York or such other Institution as they may think most expedient and to receive and pay the Interest to each of them and when in the opinion of my Executors it will be prudent and advisable to place in the hands of either of them all or any part of the said Respective legacies they are in that case authorized so to do.*

That he left Daphne and Jane, respectively, more than he left for either the church or the town's poor says a lot—perhaps, as we shall see, more than is obvious.

FAMILY

So when Thomas Peterson married his wife, she came with a legacy. But he wasn't exactly a "kept man." According to an 1884 description, "By trade he may be said to be a man of all work, yet inferior to none." Prior to the Civil War, he served on ships between Perth Amboy and Manhattan and was later described as both digging sewer trenches and maintaining lawns. In an undated newspaper clipping (presumed from between 1877 and 1884), he was quoted as saying that for "seven years I was employed by the city as janitor of the public school." An undated slip of paper found in Perth Amboy's city hall records shows that they paid him $1.62 for some kind of unidentified work. In 1870, the census even listed him as a farmer.

Since those early census records didn't include the relationship between individuals and the head of the household, it is difficult to really trace the growth of Thomas and Daphne's family. We can say, however, that they suffered the loss of at least one child. A Charles M., seven months, appears in records of deaths at Perth Amboy in the second half of 1850 as a victim of whooping cough. He was listed as the son of Thomas and "Zaph."—a clerk's or transcriber's misread abbreviation for Daphne, a name that is often surprisingly and even egregiously mangled in public records.

The 1860 census has been incorrectly indexed to show their last name as "Murray," but it also shows Thomas Peterson as a "Day Laborer" with an estate worth $600. Lucy, Thomas Peterson's then-sixty-year-old mother, is found living at Brighton House in Perth Amboy as a washerwoman. A George Mundy, age twenty-one, Samuel Mundy, age fifteen, and William Patrick, age ten, all appear as living with her. Who these Mundys and Patrick are is unclear.

By the 1870 census, their last name is spelled "Munday" but includes a Benjamin B., age eighteen; Lucy A., twelve; Alice, ten; Gilbert, seven; and a seventy-one-year-old Lucy. The fluidity of things asserts itself when this is compared with the 1880 census, where familial relationships are, at last, part of the data. Benjamin is there as Thomas and Daphne's son and Alice as their daughter. Another daughter, twenty-five-year-old Jane, also appears but was not in the 1870 record. Lucy A. also disappears. A Gilbert presents another mystery. A seven-year-old Gilbert appears on the 1870 federal census, but an under-five-year-old Gilbert is in the 1885 New Jersey state census.

There is a gap in 1890, though this is easily explained—those records were in large part destroyed by a fire in 1921.

MULATTO

If you want to get technical about it, Barack Obama is not our first "black" president. His mother was a white woman from Kansas and his father a black man from Kenya. That makes him most able to be called, literally, "African American." But, strictly speaking, it also makes him a mulatto. The distinction is, arguably, of small importance these days, but there was a time when it was serious business. The term "mulatto" generally means someone with one Caucasian parent and one African Negro parent but is often now replaced by words like "biracial" or "multiethnic" and can extend to any mixture of races. Part of the semantic shift comes from the unpleasant history of "mulatto." It is just one of several racial categories, used mostly by European colonial powers, to quantify the various combinations and mixtures between white and indigenous populations. They needed to know such details so they could say who, by law, was born to be a slave and who was not. If a Negro was viewed as inferior and justly subject to bondage, what was the status of someone who was half-Negro but also half-Caucasian? What about someone whose one parent was mulatto and the other "pure" Caucasian or Negro? The combination possibilities seemed to fascinate the English, French and Spanish bureaucrats who invented such categories as quadroons, octoroon, terceroon, griffe, sambo, etc.

Curiously—tantalizingly, perhaps—the status of Thomas Peterson and his family changed once in the U.S. censuses. In 1850, 1870 and 1900, they are indicated as "B" for "black." In 1880, however, there was a change. Thomas was still identified as "B," but Daphne and their children were marked as "M"—mulatto. Even in the hastened handwriting of the census-taker, the "M" is distinct from even the "W" entered for the whites.

It is perhaps dangerous to speculate here, but it does need to be asked—was Andrew Bell's generosity to Daphne and her sister, Jane, charitable altruism or family obligation? He would have been age sixty-three when Daphne was born. Considering he and his wife Susanna remained childless, it is possible there was some medical issue that prevented intimacy, which he sought instead with Betty—it is to be hoped, at the very least, with her consent. If he really was Daphne and Jane's father, at least he took care of them in his will. But without further evidence, assuming any could even be found, this must remain strictly an area of speculation.

CIVIL WAR

Thomas Peterson's thoughts about the outbreak of the Civil War in 1861 remain his own. But while the shooting was far away, he would have experienced at least peripherally the national trauma as it bled even into Perth Amboy.

Regiments raised from the New York area returned to Manhattan following campaigns, some catching ferries across the Hudson River to Jersey City or Perth Amboy. Perhaps Peterson saw these weary men gathered at the railway station, awaiting trains home. Some of these soldiers no doubt would have regarded Peterson as a lesser creature by virtue of the color of his skin. Yet, it is to be wondered, would either have appreciated—even in a begrudging way—that one was fighting for the betterment of the other?

It isn't known if Peterson was present, but he likely would have at least heard about an August night in 1862 when, as the *New York Times* put it, "the quiet village of Perth Amboy was all enthusiasm" over a "war meeting." Cortlandt Parker—then of Newark but representing a family name going back to eighteenth-century Perth Amboy—gave an "eloquent appeal" that the town do its part in raising the 600,000-men national quota called for by President Lincoln. By the end of the night, the town passed a resolution to raise money to "thoroughly outfit and pay liberal bounty to such as should volunteer."

Much of Perth Amboy seems to have supported the Union cause, though it was by no means unanimous. By 1865, the *New York Times* was lamenting how troops—some coming home for the first time in as many as three years—were received in New York and New Jersey not by a grateful public but by a lone government agent, who led them to a hot meal in dingy barracks. Perhaps such ambivalence resulted from weariness with the war. Troops coming and going, no matter how gallant, had by then become a commonplace sight.

When the war came to its bloody conclusion in 1865, it brought with it for people like the Petersons the prospect of hope for the future. That same year, the United States adopted the Thirteenth Amendment to the Constitution. At last, once and for all, slavery would be abolished in the land. But if anyone were under any illusions that the transformation would be easy, the assassination of President Abraham Lincoln in April of the same year would disabuse them. It is to be wondered how Thomas and his family received the news.

Still, tomorrow must have seemed a little brighter after all the bloodshed and misery. Perhaps such beliefs inspired Thomas and Daphne when they decided to cash in on that legacy from Andrew Bell and buy a home all their own.

A HOUSE ALL THEIR OWN

We don't know where they had been living—the census records didn't record such data yet. There is, however, reason to believe they may have lived with the family of James Lawrence Kearny—who appears most often in the records as "J.L." Born in 1846, J.L. was the son of U.S. Navy commodore Lawrence Kearny (1780–1868), who was perhaps best known for beginning negotiations with China in the early 1840s that opened the nation to trade with the United States. The commodore may not have made many friends in town, however. It seems he sued the city over a street re-grading project that meant he had to add steps from his door to the street. In Katherine Beekman's 1918 reminiscences of her girlhood in the Perth Amboy of the 1850s, she recalled that the commodore, when walking the streets, had the unpleasant habit of muttering the word "damn" over and over again.

His son, however, was more popular and, as will be seen, would play a pivotal role in Peterson's voting.

Andrew Bell's great-nephew, William Paterson (1817–1899, not to be confused with the earlier William Paterson), had been tasked with administering some of the trusts from his late great-uncle's will—including the $500 left to Daphne. A Princeton graduate (1835), Paterson was admitted to the bar in 1838, but thanks to his being "of independent means," he didn't need to practice law until mid-life, when he opened offices in Newark and Perth Amboy. In 1852, he married Salvadora Meade, a Spanish-born woman living in Philadelphia. The 1870 census finds them living in Perth Amboy with their sixteen-year-old daughter Emily and William's twin brother, Stephen Van Renssalaer Paterson. Over the years between 1846 and 1878, William served as Perth Amboy's mayor and president of New Jersey's College of Electors—particularly noted for having been the one to cast the state's vote for George B. McClellan over Abraham Lincoln in the 1864 presidential election.

On May 10, 1849, Paterson had bought a plot of land off Commerce Street from the Perth Amboy Manufacturing Company. When Thomas and Daphne Peterson were looking for a house, Paterson sold them this property and even built them a house in return for the $500 principle of the legacy. We know this thanks to the deed record, which described "the home thereon having been built for the use of Daphne Mundy from a legacy…by the late will and testament of Andrew Bell."

It was in this house that Thomas Peterson was living when the opportunity came to make history.

Negro Suffrage

Every now and then—usually on an anniversary of Peterson's vote—some reporter, or even a historian, will celebrate how Thomas Peterson was the first African American to vote in the United States.

Well…not exactly.

In many of the first state constitutions drafted in and after 1776, no mention is even made of *any* limitations on the rights of suffrage, let alone racial ones. Others used broad enough language that neither race nor gender was identified as either impediments or requirements. As late as 1790, of the original thirteen states, only Virginia, Georgia and South Carolina specifically limited voting based on race. In many cases, it seems the authors were just trying to throw up a quick framework of government to replace the provincial versions they were hoping to shortly overthrow. There would be time enough to revise things later. Assuming, of course, that the point was not rendered moot by losing the war and them all being hanged as traitors.

In New Jersey's case, the constitution was drafted in a particularly harried five days and ratified in the following two. The framers were, metaphorically speaking, looking over their collective shoulders across the Hudson River, to where the British had taken over New York. New Jersey seemed next and was teetering on the verge of civil collapse. The constitution was more of a temporary expedient, long on rhetoric and short on considered details. When it came to setting the requirements for suffrage, Article IV declared:

> *That all inhabitants of this Colony, of full age, who are worth fifty pounds proclamation money, clear estate in the same, and have resided within the county in which they claim a vote for twelve months immediately preceding the election, shall be entitled to vote for Representatives in Council and Assembly; and also for all other public officers, that shall be elected by the people of the county at large.*

It may have been an oversight, but there was no specific limitation based on either race or gender. As long as you had lived long enough where you intended to vote and had enough personal wealth, there was no lawful reason a woman or Negro couldn't cast a ballot. Between 1787 and 1788, when the U.S. Constitution was up for ratification, both blacks and whites are known to have voted on the question.

Once the immediate crisis of the war had passed, legislators in many states got down to working on "fixing" their respective constitutions, until by 1850, twenty-five of the thirty-one states existing at the time had specific racial limitations on voting in their respective documents.

Amazingly, despite evident shortcomings—such as the lack of provisions for future amendment—the New Jersey Constitution survived unchanged until 1844. At last, a constitutional convention was convened to rewrite the whole thing, complete with language limiting suffrage to "every white male citizen of the United States, of the age of twenty-one years, who shall have been a resident of this State one year, and of the county, in which he claims his vote five months, next before the election, shall be entitled to vote for all officers that now are, or hereafter may be elective by the people."

So what made Thomas Peterson's vote historically significant is that it wasn't cast under any state constitution but rather by the authority of the U.S. Constitution, which overrode all the rest. New Jersey and other states were left to rewrite their constitutions to be in line with the new law of the land.

INCLUSION AND PARTICIPATION

Someplace had to have the first election after March 30, 1870. As luck would have it, of all the places in the country, it would be in Perth Amboy, New Jersey. It is perhaps fitting that this election wasn't really a partisan fight between Democratic or Republican candidates—it was about the form of self-government that the good citizens of Perth Amboy wanted.

So, it was by dumb luck that Thomas Peterson became the first African American to vote under the Fifteenth Amendment. He could have cast his ballot and gone back to work, disappearing into history as a footnote.

But he didn't.

In a perfect world, Peterson wouldn't have had anything more to prove than any other man. But he didn't live in a perfect world—he lived in the acutely racially divisive world of 1870. He lived in a world where there were plenty of people who would have loved nothing more than for him to have done something stupid—anything that they could point to and lament the day "those people" were given the vote. I think he understood that, likely through a combination of innate acuity and the influence of the Eagleswood progressives. Peterson was, in fact, a hardworking, God-fearing and sober man. True, a lazy, drunken heathen would still be just as entitled to the franchise. But as abolition turned into civil rights advocacy, he was an honestly respectable poster boy for the cause.

While Perth Amboy seems to have been something of an enclave of progressivism, not everyone was happy to see a dark hand drop a ballot into the ballot box. Peterson liked to tell of how one white man, upon seeing him vote, ripped up his own ballot, declaring the franchise worthless if a Negro could do it—adding that the man didn't vote again for the next ten years.

But there is a complexity to how even Peterson's champions saw him. There were in America at the time many whites who saw slavery as a cruel and unchristian practice and were glad to see it abolished. But they wouldn't necessarily go so far as to see a black man or woman as their equals. During the now-famous Lincoln-Douglas debates of 1858, then-senatorial candidate Abraham Lincoln argued that slavery violated "natural law"—that it was unnatural for any man to own another. Yet he also soft-pedaled the argument for Stephen Douglas's supporters by adding that he didn't necessarily see the Negro as his social equal or entitled to the full rights of citizenship. It was the extreme of slavery that he objected to but not necessarily the perceptions of inherent inequity that underlay it. It was possible, Lincoln was arguing in what may have been political pragmatism, to abolish slavery without automatically granting social and political equity.

There was an undeniable paternalism in how some regarded Peterson—he was the proverbial "credit to his race." A nice guy, to be sure, but still apart from his white neighbors. Nevertheless, he used his newfound local celebrity to participate in the political life of the city, proving that the inclusion of a black man in such affairs wouldn't herald the end of civilization as they knew it.

"As I advanced to the polls one man offered me a ticket bearing the words 'revised charter,' and another one marked, 'no charter,'" Peterson later told a reporter about his voting experience. "I thought I would not vote to give up the charter after holding it so long; so I chose a revised charter ballot. Our side won the election by a vote of 230 to 63 and I may mention as a coincidence that I was afterward appointed one of a committee of seven to revise the charter."

Not only did Peterson get to vote on the question at hand, but he also was able to participate in the process of actually revising the charter he had voted to keep. There had been no objections raised to his inclusion. As of this writing, minutes or other records of that process and what Peterson may have contributed are still wanting. But summary treatments of his life include how he was named a delegate to the conventions held by Middlesex County Republicans on more than one occasion and served as a juror in county courts. Again, Peterson scholars are still working on finding clues that might shed light on his activities. On the local level anyway, Peterson was participating in civic life in a way that would have been unthinkable for his parents' generation.

But what was really happening here? Aside from the gentleman who tore up his ballot, were Perth Amboy and Middlesex County really infused with such a progressive spirit that they would accept a black man in such positions? I think there are probably three dynamics at work here. One is that there really were some very liberal-minded folks who were fully prepared to shed the cultural biases of their ancestors and see a black man as their brother—certainly Marcus and Rebecca Spring were prepared to go that far.

But most of his white neighbors and friends probably accepted him more provisionally. It's worth noting as a parallel that in many New Jersey suburbs into the early twentieth century, black families moved in and never really suffered the kinds of bigotry present elsewhere, particularly the Deep South. Were white folks in the suburban Garden State just more enlightened? Well, to a point. One or two families was one thing, and whites could indeed feel enlightened in accepting them as neighbors and friends. But where it became dozens of black families, racial divides became wider and deeper. One black man was fine—particularly one as nice and respectable as ol' Tom Mundy—even as a delegate to a political convention or sitting in judgment as a juror. Even when other blacks in Perth Amboy showed up at the polling places, it was fine. But how far could ol' Tom Mundy have really pushed that warm, fuzzy feeling? Where was the tipping point between where inclusion felt morally good and where it started to feel like a threat to the established order?

We actually have something of an answer in the voting returns of a city election held on April 18, 1879. "Thomas Mundy" appears as running for councilman. Thomas Peterson was the only "Thomas Mundy" living in Perth Amboy at the time—it is worth noting that he used the Mundy name, the name by which most of the white community likely best knew him. He received just 2 votes. The winner, Chester Smith, received 274. But at least Peterson did better than Pat Carr or John Adair. They just had a single vote each—likely their own.

A third dynamic at play was probably simple opportunism. Whatever one thought of Negro suffrage before, they were a potential voting block now. They were the beneficiaries, after all, of Republican policies that resulted in the three-amendment set that had just turned them into full-fledged citizens. To some degree, Thomas Peterson was a political commodity that could be leveraged to court the new black vote. He seems to have been a sincerely decent human being, something that translated in the game of politics to mean unthreatening to white voters still leery of Negro inclusion in civic life. Exactly how much Republican Party leaders made use of this isn't yet clear. Perhaps when more about his participation in their conventions comes to light, we will better understand this aspect of the story.

Interestingly, the one clear example of using the Thomas Peterson brand for political gain comes not from the Republicans but the Democrats. In 1900, they were fielding William Jennings Bryan (1860–1925) and Adlai Stevenson (1835–1914) as presidential candidates against the incumbent Republican, William McKinley. For Bryan, a liberal Democrat, this was the second of what would be three failed attempts. He stood opposed to American imperialism and the hold the gold standard had on the nation's economy. Something about his platform struck a chord with Peterson, and he came out in support of Bryan as offering the best deal for the workingman, white or black. In a small announcement appearing in the *Omaha World Herald*, the Democrats seized the opportunity to crow about how the first Negro voter under the Fifteenth Amendment—and a lifelong Republican to boot—supported *their* candidates.

It would have been interesting to have a more detailed account of what Peterson thought of the politics at stake. But he would have certainly agreed with Bryan on one score—prohibition. Peterson told a reporter in an undated article that he had belonged to the prohibitionist movement for around fifteen years by then and saw rum as the curse of his race.

Indeed, in an article covering the Prohibition Party's convention to nominate a "General Fisk" for New Jersey governor in 1886, the *Bridgeton Evening News* made special note that Peterson was there as a delegate from Perth Amboy. "They won't settle the rum question," he complained about the Republican Party, "they fool us every year, and I'm done with them." Evidently, he felt so strongly about the issue that he had left the Republicans. Clearly, it seemed Peterson was his own man when it came to politics.

"A Token on the Freedman's Coat"

The year 1884 was also a presidential election year—and an important one at that. Before the Civil War, a pro-slavery faction was dominant in the Democratic Party, counseling an immediate peace deal with the Confederates once war came. They called themselves "Peace Democrats," but Republicans branded them the "Copperheads," an allusion to what they saw as a snake-like treachery. The last time a Democrat sat in the White House before 1884 was James Buchanan in a heated 1856 election—the beginning of a Democratic losing streak that would last six election cycles and remains the longest such streak in U.S. history to date.

By 1876, however, with abolition no longer a question and other issues asserting themselves, the Democrats had an opportunity to recast their image. Republicans disparaged this new breed as "Bourbon Democrats," mocking what seemed to them like old-fashioned ideas. Bourbon Democrats embraced big business interests—banking and railroads in particular—but stood against giving them subsidies and favored letting competition drive things. They promoted a laissez-faire capitalism and opposed American adventurism abroad while embracing the gold standard and seeking to reform political bossism—particularly New York's Boss Tweed machine. In 1884, these new Democrats had their best chance of recapturing the White House with a former governor of New York who was born in Caldwell, New Jersey: Grover Cleveland.

It would be a close win for Cleveland and a short-lived triumph for his party. Four years later, he lost to Benjamin Harrison in even more of a squeaker—Cleveland won the popular vote but lost in the Electoral College, something that wouldn't happen again until the 2000 election. It had been a rough and nasty campaign, with Cleveland admitting to having fathered a child out of wedlock. But in Perth Amboy, anyway, there would be an interesting rally of bipartisanship around Thomas Peterson.

Whatever the motivations, it had remained a point of pride for Perth Amboy that the first Negro voter under the Fifteenth Amendment was one of their own. Peterson himself enjoyed a degree of local celebrity and respect. So it would have come as an unpleasant surprise to discover that *another* black man was claiming the same title. In April 1884, the *Princeton Press* ran a short article:

> *Mose* [short for Moses] *is known far and wide as a professor of music. He goes as far as Atlantic City this season, and has officiated at 125 sociables. By the way, he wears a medal conferred upon him by the people of New Jersey, in honor of being the first colored citizen to vote under the Fifteenth amendment in this State.*

Not a lot is known yet about Moses Schenck beyond the brief data-points gleaned from the U.S. Census. In 1860, he was a twenty-two-year-old waiter. An 1863 draft record describes him as a twenty-five-year-old unmarried laborer. In 1870, he had married a woman twelve years his senior named Mary and was working as a hotel waiter. The 1880 census confirms his occupation as a musician. Mary was a cook, and they lived on Hulfish Street in Princeton. He died December 27, 1890, at age fifty-seven.

While Peterson enjoyed his status, he did not want it if he had not honestly deserved it. He asked that a committee of citizens be formed to investigate Schenck's claim. It was said that Peterson selected them personally. Of the two men who urged him to vote that day, Marcus Spring had died in 1874, but J.L. Kearny was still around, so he was tapped to head the committee. The rest consisted of local politician Patrick Convery, who had been manning the polls when Peterson cast his ballot; ex-mayor and then-judge William Paterson (the same William Paterson who had sold Daphne the land and house); and Alderman John Fothergill. All were Democrats. Balancing out the committee for the Republicans was Collector of the Port J.L. Boggs, ex-mayor and banker U.B. Watson and City Treasurer I.T. Golding.

They wrote to the Princeton newspaper's editor, asking for further explanation, to which he replied:

[Moses Schenck] *was born in Princeton, and quite an intelligent man. On the 4th of April, 1870, Monday, at the annual election for borough officers…Moses Schenck, was the first of about 100 colored voters to cast a ballot. The medal referred to reads: "Moses Schenck, First Voter under the Fifteenth Amendment, Princeton, N.J., April 4, 1870." I gave Mose [sic] the medal, and by it did not mean to claim for him more than he was the FIRST VOTER IN PRINCETON under the Fifteenth Amendment. The story of his actually being the first voter under the Amendment, has come up under a misapprehension. I have just spoken to Mose about it, and he says he did not set a very high value on Peterson's claim, for he only voted on a question of a charter amendment, while here, it was the regular election for Mayor, Council, etc. Mose is very proud of his medal, and, undoubtedly, shows it very freely to strangers, and probably claims more than he has a right to.*

As far as the committee was concerned, the non-partisan nature did not affect Peterson's priority—indeed, it was a badge of honor. If Schenck had voted April 4 and Peterson on March 31, it was clear that the honor belonged to Perth Amboy's resident. Their civic pride had been challenged and, they decided, if Schenck had a medal for being first in Princeton, certainly Thomas Peterson should have one for being first in the entire nation!

After making sure there were no other elections held the same day that could more seriously challenge Peterson's priority, they set to work organizing the striking of a gold medallion. They raised seventy dollars for the purpose—not a minor sum in those days. It consisted of a two-inch-wide gold bar on which was imprinted "Thomas Peterson, Perth Amboy." Hanging from it by two chains was a two-inch-diameter round medallion featuring a profile bust of Abraham Lincoln—interestingly, a younger version, sans beard. On the reverse, it read:

PRESENTED BY CITIZENS OF
PERTH AMBOY, N. J.
TO
THOMAS PETERSON,
THE FIRST COLORED VOTER IN
THE UNITED STATES UNDER
THE FIFTEENTH AMENDMENT,
AT AN ELECTION HELD IN
THAT CITY, MARCH 31, 1870

It would be presented to him on May 30, 1884—Decoration Day, the post–Civil War precursor to Memorial Day.

PATERNALISM

Sitting in the audience to witness the presentation of the medal to her son was eighty-four-year-old Lucy. Perhaps she thought back to her own life in bondage as a young woman and wondered what her enslaved mother might have thought of it all.

It was a big step for people who looked like her and her son. But it was also a step for the white people in the audience around her. They were pinning a medal to a man's coat for doing something that in other parts of the country they would be putting a noose around his neck for. It was fortunate in the extreme that the first election was in Perth Amboy, New Jersey—a place where there was an element of the white community that would encourage that first vote and a black man of solid personal character to not only cast the ballot but also embrace the role that act imposed upon him. Had it been a less sympathetic state, perhaps that first voter would have wound up dead. Those who followed Peterson's example in other parts of the country would do so with a greater degree of personal risk. Perth Amboy, at least, showed how it could work.

Yet even here, in that shining moment when the community was taking pride in Peterson as one of their own, they couldn't help but keep at least one foot on the side of old attitudes.

A former mayor, James M. Chapman, said a few words, followed by "some short but very appropriate remarks" by Reverend Dr. Stevenson. But it was William Paterson who was selected to speak on behalf of the committee. He should have taken his lead from Reverend Dr. Stevenson. His remarks were longwinded, convoluted and, at least from a modern perspective, of questionable appropriateness. He meandered, for some odd reason, through a commentary on the sylvan founding of Perth Amboy, hoping, perhaps, to make the point of how much an advance in civilization Peterson's vote was by contrast. He even included long, melodramatic stanzas of florid poetry.

But it was when introducing how Moses Schenck made his claim that he betrayed the still-paternalistic way even those there to honor Peterson viewed him. He told his long-suffering audience, "There is a common saying familiar to all that a darkey is under the woodpile," in reference to Schenck's presumed effort to steal the other black man's thunder. The phrase was used—often with an even more offensive word than "darkey"—to mean a sneak. Later, on the same subject, he interjected an odd, almost childish verse: "So it came out not long ago that / 'Another of the colored clan / To make a rhyme, say black and tan,' / living in a University town of high repute where the same dark hue was interwoven in the academic flag…" For some reason, the fact that Princeton University's colors were orange and, specifically, black was also of relevance to Paterson.

One has to wonder what was going through Thomas Peterson's mind as he heard words like "darkey" being bandied about, albeit in what Paterson no doubt thought was a well-meaning—even complimentary—context. It probably wasn't anything he hadn't heard plenty of times before.

A pamphlet of the proceedings was produced to record the event for posterity, with copies being sent to both Trenton and Washington, D.C. In the introduction, however, there may be the best (or worst) example of the duality of the progressive and the paternalistic present that day. In what was intended as a sincere compliment, the unnamed author wrote how the well-respected Peterson "no doubt will remain quite an institution until called to go where Uncle Ned and all the good darkies go."

Aside from yet more liberal use of the term "darkies," there is also the implied conclusion of a separate heaven for blacks and whites. Even by 1923, when local historian Harold E. Pickersgill was writing about Peterson for his history column in the *Perth Amboy Evening News*, he described him this way:

> *Tom was a simple hearted, honest man, a perfect representation of the typical northern negro who was willing to work, knew his place and who did his best to earn the respect of those about him, regardless of color.*

Later in the same piece, Pickersgill says of him:

> *Tom knew the importance of the honor that unexpectedly came to him, through no effort of his own, and whether it was in digging sewer trenches or working about the lawns that he earned his way, there was a certain dignity about him which indicated even to those who saw him for the first time that there was something out of the common about him. In the history of his race after emancipation, his name should have a prominent place and in his life before and after that event of March 31, 1871 [sic] there was nothing that would add aught but credit to the record.*

In other words, he was a credit to his race. The community genuinely liked him, sang his praises and celebrated his lucky vote with seventy dollars' worth of gold.

But he was still the "other."

Regardless of intentions, phrases like "the good darkies" and "knew his place" made me cringe when I first read them. But, again, one must step back for a moment and consider the full context of the bigger picture. In the decade after Peterson cast his vote in 1870, over six hundred black people were lynched or otherwise killed in racially motivated murders in the United States. When they gave him his medal in 1884, it was in a period of relative calm between 1880 and 1889, when the number dropped to under two hundred. But that was only because of an 1871 Civil Rights Act, which then-president Ulysses S. Grant pushed through to effectively dismantle the KKK—at least for a while. By the period between 1920 and 1929, inclusive of when Pickersgill was writing his column, the number of lynchings had jumped back to over five hundred.

Against that metric, what happened in Perth Amboy—for all its imperfection of tone—was truly remarkable.

LATER YEARS

While to modern ears, William Paterson seems to have prattled on ad nauseum, Harold Pickersgill apparently had a different impression, calling it "one of those graceful speeches for which Judge Paterson was more than locally famed." But he did have one little bit of verse that more gracefully captured the moment:

> *And so we meet to decorate,*
> *By token on the Freedman's coat,*
> *The man who was in any State,*
> *The first to cast a Freedman's vote.*

It's said that Thomas Peterson was proud of his medal and never considered himself properly dressed for services at St. Peter's without it affixed to the left breast of his shiny Prince Albert–style coat. Boots, pants and a prized old silk hat completed his ensemble. Within the collections of the Perth Amboy Public Library is a photograph of Peterson. It has been copied and reproduced ever since, from his obituaries to modern online histories. But in this original print, the details are wonderfully crisp. This is Peterson as a mature man, some wrinkles around his keen eyes and gray in his hair and the mustache and beard combo he sports. He looks off over the right shoulder of the viewer. He looks proud and self-possessed but not in a hard or unapproachable way—perhaps there is a faint smile under the mustache. There is definitely an air of that dignity Pickersgill said was so apparent, even to strangers who first met him.

He wears a medium-toned suit jacket and matching vest, a shirt with light vertical stripes and a dark tie with small light dots. A chain is fixed to a lower vest button, leading down out of the picture, likely linking with a pocketwatch. Just above it, pinned to the left breast of the vest, is his medal, Lincoln's profile just visible if you look close enough. So we know it was taken in 1884 or later. He would have been, at minimum, sixty years old.

If this were a made-for-TV movie, we might zoom in on those eyes here, fade to black and start rolling the credits.

But the rest of Peterson's story—like so much else here—isn't quite so simple. While he enjoyed a degree of local celebrity and respect—even

Thomas Peterson wearing the medal he was given by the city of Perth Amboy in honor of his historic vote. *Courtesy of the Perth Amboy Free Public Library.*

prestige as a delegate to Republican conventions and as a juror—there was always only going to be so far he was ever really going to go in life as a black man. He was better off than many others, of course. Thanks to the legacy left to Daphne, they owned their own home at 9 Commerce Lane, a dead-end, unpaved lane running south from Commerce Street. It was a modest but certainly respectable house. Though no longer standing, Sanborn Fire Insurance maps indicate a two-story wood frame structure with a one-story lean-to out back where the kitchen was. Local historian John Dyke found a vintage photograph where part of the Petersons' house can be seen in the background. Thanks to that, we know it was a front-gable, board and batten clad building.

Peterson continued to work, being appointed superintendent of the new elementary school building—a janitorial job but probably better paying than the random handyman gigs he seems to have otherwise been depending on.

Yet financial security was not to be his in the declining years of his life. The first blow came on November 23, 1891, when Daphne—his wife of some forty-seven years—passed away. Fortunately, he had an extended family to comfort him. But then around 1899, the seventy-five-year-old Peterson

In the background of this photograph, taken of the grander home next door, may be glimpsed a small portion of the house Thomas and Daphne Peterson shared on Commerce Lane. *Courtesy of John Kerry Dyke.*

found his eyesight failing him, leaving him partially blind and unable to work—and, apparently, leaving the house he had shared with Daphne too much to deal with on his own. With his daughters Alice G. Peterson and Jane Johnson with her husband, Alfred, also being named on the deed, the Commerce Lane house was sold to St. Peter's Church for $900.

The 1900 census finds Peterson living with his daughter and son-in-law and his four grandchildren, all still at 9 Commerce Lane—evidently, the church permitted their old parishioner to remain in the house with his family. He had become an object of charity. A February 26, 1901 article from the *Philadelphia Inquirer* described how a group of Perth Amboy businessmen had formed a committee to help raise money to keep the "aged colored man" they described as having been "out of work for some time…feeble and ill, and has been in actual want." Perhaps saddest of all was how it would later be remembered that he at times was forced to pawn his prized voting medal.

The end came in early February 1904. He had been unwell, and a doctor had to be called on the fourth of February. At 5:20 p.m., at age seventy-nine, Thomas Peterson passed away at home.

In the archives of St. Peter's, there is the accounts book of Fred F. Fox, the undertaker who buried Thomas Peterson. It is billed to "Ms. Peterson," presumably Alice, given that Jane would have been Ms. Johnson. Their father had a "Polished Casket, Handles & Plate trimmed Complete," costing $35. The outer pine case was $5, two coaches were had at $6, and the hearse for $7. Opening the grave cost $5 and use of the church $2. The service of the undertaker and assistant was $5, bringing the grand total to $65—roughly $1,600 in 2010 dollars. It was paid off in two installments, one of $60 and one of $5, in cash.

He was laid to rest at St. Peter's Church graveyard on February 7, 1904, at two o'clock on a Saturday afternoon. Some fifty people packed the pews to hear Reverend J.L. Lancaster speak and the women's choir sing two hymns. The *Perth Amboy Evening News* sought fit to note in the first paragraph that at least half the audience was white.

It also noted that two of his brothers were in attendance, one from Perth Amboy and the other a justice of the peace from Plainfield, New Jersey.

H.

There is something curious about Peterson's death certificate. Both he and his father are identified as "Thomas H. Peterson." At first blush, it almost seems like a typo—certainly it would be "M." for Mundy? But then the "H." appears again in the undertaker's accounts book. Some later historian or genealogist was also evidently confused by it. There are some notes on the page, made in pencil, and hash marks lightly over the "H." as if to correct it, perhaps to read "M." Then there is the 1900 deed that conveyed the Commerce Lane house to St. Peter's Church—once more he is identified as "Thomas H. Peterson."

Once could be a mistake. Twice, perhaps coincidence. But three times?

The mystery of the "H." is solved by the obituary that appeared in the *Perth Amboy Evening News*. It begins, "Thomas Henry Peterson, seventy-nine years old, the first colored voter in the United States..."

He's known these days as Thomas Mundy Peterson, but that combination *never* appears in any contemporary records. The closest was the cover of the pamphlet produced describing the 1884 award of the voting medal—and that reads "Thomas Peterson-Mundy." But in all other contemporary records found thus far, he is either Thomas Mundy or Thomas Peterson.

It is perhaps telling that the "H." emerges in documents from the end of Peterson's life—when his children are involved. They were part of the 1900 deed transaction. They would have given the information for the death certificate and to the undertaker, and to the hometown newspaper who published his obituary on the front page.

It may be hyperbole to call "Mundy" Peterson's slave name. Certainly it would be inaccurate—Peterson was never a slave. But the inclusion of the Mundy name as part of his identity is evocative of the paternalism under which his generation had labored. Perhaps—and this is speculation—at the dawn of the twentieth century, his kids thought it was high time that their father assert his own identity as a free, independent human being named Thomas Henry Peterson.

FATE OF THE MEDAL

After lamenting their loss, Perth Amboy's citizens remembered that gold medal they had given him—what, many wanted to know, had become of it? In a story worthy of a front-page article in the *Perth Amboy Evening Times*, it was announced on February 6, 1904, that it was safe and sound—albeit not in the hands of Peterson's heirs, who had no idea where it had gone. Peterson had kept it locked away in an old seaman's chest from his days on the water.

Exactly what happened to the medal is a little sketchy.

In this initial account, Peterson was in need of money and decided to pawn his prized possession one more time. He gave it to a W.D. Vorhees, who turned it over to local businessman and philanthropist John H. Gregory. Gregory loaned Peterson twenty-five dollars for the medal.

In a second front-page article on the tenth, however, the story had changed a little. Gregory clarified that he hadn't loaned any money to Peterson and that Peterson had told Vorhees to *sell* the medal. Vorhees, in turn, handed it over to Perth Amboy's then-mayor, C.K. Seaman, who was on his way to Manhattan to the assay office to sell it for cash—after which, it would likely have been melted down. He happened to bump into Gregory, who immediately bought it. If the city ever had a museum or such proper place to display it, he would give it them, but for now, he would keep it in his personal safe.

There are two important differences between the stories. In the first account, Peterson was only pawning the medal for a loan. Technically, Gregory would not own it but was holding it as collateral against the loan. If the family had come up with the money to pay him back, they could have retrieved the medal. But in the second story, Peterson wanted to sell it—relinquishing ownership to whomever bought it. And that was now Gregory, who looked like the hero of the day, having saved this piece of Perth Amboy—and American—history from being melted down and lost forever.

It is, of course, possible that the first story did indeed lack all the details. Or perhaps Gregory modified things to assume possession of the medal. Would Thomas Peterson have really sold it, as opposed to pawn it as he had before? It is perhaps worth noting that there does not appear to have been any attempts by Peterson's heirs to get the medal back or any compensation for it. And evidently, at least daughter Jane could have used the money. When she died on January 7, 1910, she was a fifty-year-old widow. "Mrs. Johnston [*sic*] lived on charity for several years," her obituary said, adding, "Her father died in poverty five years ago."

Whatever the case, the medal eventually found its way to Harold Pickersgill and then into the Charles F. Heartman's Negro Culture Collection. Heartman was an antiquarian book dealer who specialized in materials relating to the African American experience. St. Peter's Reverend George H. Boyd attempted to buy the medal back at one point for Perth Amboy, but a deal never materialized, to the disappointment of William McGinnis, who wrote that while the reverend "offered to pay a good price for it," the "new owner refused to sell it to the church." When Heartman died in 1948, parts of his vast collection were broken up (much of it is now at South Texas University) and the lots were auctioned off, including the medal. It was bought by Xavier University of Louisiana, where it remains today. These days, Perth Amboy's history community laments that it is so far from home but take some comfort from the fact that Xavier is, fittingly, an African American university.

Peterson's name, while not as well known as some others of the civil rights movement, is still recalled with some pride in and around Perth Amboy. That elementary school where he was superintendent is now the Thomas M. Peterson Elementary School. Apparently Peterson's kin were unable to afford a grave marker, and the plot remained unmarked for over fifty years. Members of St. Peter's raised the funds to at last commemorate both Thomas and Daphne (who does have a marble marker that has had to be repaired after breaking in half). While Daphne had a gravestone, her husband for many years did not. On November 1, 1959, a flat granite marker was dedicated, reading:

Here Lies The Body Of
THOMAS PETERSON
FIRST NEGRO VOTER IN THE UNITED STATES
UNDER THE FIFTEENTH AMENDMENT
AT AN ELECTION HELD IN PERTH AMBOY
March 31, 1870
Member of
A Committee To Revise The City Charter
Born October 6, 1824
Died February 4, 1904
His Wife
DAPHNE REEVE PETERSON
Born October 2, 1820
Died November 23, 1891

In attendance at the dedication were his grandson Alfonso Peterson and his wife, along with their daughter, Althea.

In one more acknowledgement, on April 3, 1998, the New Jersey legislature passed a resolution that henceforth March 31 be known throughout the state as Thomas Mundy Peterson Day.

NEVER-ENDING STORY

Okay—*now* the fade to black and roll the credits, right?

Well, no. The story doesn't really end here either. As late as 1965, Congress had to pass an act to remind Americans that it still wasn't acceptable to deny citizens the right to vote because of race. Even today, as I write this at the start of the 2012 election cycle, allegations remain of attempts to make it more difficult to vote in non-white neighborhoods.

In 1970, at the 100th anniversary of Peterson's vote, Marcia Chamber of the *News Tribune* asked several of Perth Amboy's business and civic leaders, "Can the black man achieve full equality in this country?" It was a time still reverberating from the race riots that made Newark a front-page news item just three years earlier. Pessimism was high in both the black and white answers. The evolution continues.

All things considered, Thomas Peterson's act of voting was as simple as dropping a slip of paper through a slot. Maybe it took a minute at most. Still, consider for a moment all that had taken place to make that moment possible, and the promise it represented for what might come after. It was, ultimately, just one step in an ongoing evolution.

Yet, in that simple act, Thomas Peterson made history.

Bibliography

CHAPTER 1

Asbury Park Evening Press. "Clouds of Dust from West Cast Pall over Seaboard." May 12, 1934, 1.

Daily Home News. "Dr. Lipman Plans U.S. Soil Survey." May 11, 1934, 1.

Egan, Timothy. *The Worst Hard Time: The Untold Story of Those Who Survived the Great American Dust Bowl.* New York: Houghton Mifflin Harcourt, 2006.

Elizabeth Daily Journal. "Fear for Crops Grows as Dust Blots U.S. Area." May 11, 1934, 1.

Myers, Fred. "$2,000,000,000 Daily Crop Loss in Giant Dust Storm." *Paterson Evening News.* May 11, 1934, 1.

New York Times. "Huge Dust Cloud, Blown 1,500 Miles, Dims City 5 House." May 12, 1934, 1.

————. "Wheat Forecast Dips 170,000,000 BU. Under Average." May 11, 1934, 1.

CHAPTER 2

Alder, Ken. *The Lie Detectors: The History of an American Obsession*. New York: Free Press, 2007.

Bertram, Lucille. Personal email, January 12, 2009.

Brean, Herbert. "'Hidden Sell' Technique Is Almost Here." *Life*, March 31, 1958, 104.

Crandall, Kelly B. "Invisible Commercials and Hidden Persuaders: James M. Vicary and the Subliminal Advertising Controversy of 1957." Undergraduate honors thesis, University of Florida Department of History, Gainesville, Florida, April 12, 2006.

Fukuda, Kyosuke. "Eye Blinks: A New Indices for the Detection of Deception." *International Journal of Psychophysiology*, 40, no. 3 (April 2001): 239–45.

Henderson, Carter. "A Blessing or a Bane? TV Ads You'd See Without Knowing It." *Wall Street Journal*, September 13, 1957.

Moskowitz, Eva S. *In Therapy We Trust: America's Obsession with Self-Fulfillment*. Baltimore: Johns Hopkins University Press, 2001.

www.fortleefilm.org/history.html.

CHAPTER 3

Newman, M.S. "Train Talk. Carrier System for End-to-End Communication Speeds Up Freights on Pennsy Branch Line." *Railroad Magazine*, October 1944.

CHAPTER 4

New York Times. "Jerseyan First to Report News." November 3, 1957.

CHAPTER 5

Frasca, Ralph. "'At the Sign of the Bribe Refused': The Constitutional Courant and the Stamp Tax, 1765." *New Jersey History.* 107 (Fall–Winter 1989): 21–39.

Ketchum, Richard M. *Divided Loyalties: How The Revolution Came to New York*. New York: Henry Holt and Company, 2002.

O'Callaghan, M.D., E.B., ed. "Documents Relative to the Colonial History of the State of New York; Procured in Holland, England and France, by John Romeyn Brodhead, Esq., Agent, under and by virtue of an Act of the Legislature entitled 'An Act to Appoint and Agent to Procure and transcribe Documents in Europe Relating to the Colonial History of the State,' passed May 2, 1839." Albany, NY: Weed, Parsons and Company, Printers, 1855. Vol. VII.

Thomas, Isaiah, and Marcus A. McCorison, ed. *The History of Printing in America with a Biography of Printers and an Account of Newspapers*. New York: Weathervane Publishers, Inc., 1970.

Wilcox, William, ed., et al. *The Papers of Benjamin Franklin, Volume 12, January 1 through December 31, 1765*. New Haven, CT: Yale University Press, 1968.

CHAPTER 6

Arkansas State Press. "OPM Employm't Picture Untrue Says NAACP." August 8, 1941, 1.

Bradshaw, G.A. "Know New Jersey—No. 39." *Trenton Evening Times,* October 2, 1941, 10.

Cunningham, John T. "Newark." 1988, New Jersey Historical Society, Newark, NJ.

Francis, Devon. "Air Traffic Cops May Not Be Such a Fantastic Idea." *Springfield Republican*, November 10, 1940, 13.

Harding, Richard T.F. "The Byproduct." *Plain Dealer*, January 9, 1940, 20.

Harrison, Dale. "New York." *Seattle Daily Times*, August 28, 1940, 6.

Jewish Chronicle. "Community Pays Raymond Tribute." October 12, 1928, 1.

———. "'Y' Participates in USO Activities." September 4, 1942, 1.

J.T.K. "Untermann, Silverstein, Parsonnet, Schotl and, Gansler Among Jewish Appointees to City Posts." *Jewish Chronicle*, May 23, 1941, 1, 3.

Kilgallen, Dorothy. "The Voice of Broadway." *Trenton Evening Times*. September 19, 1940, 10.

Levinstone, Aaron. "Ellenstein—The Fighting Mayor." *Jewish Chronicle*, April 25, 1941, 1, 3.

Lurie, Maxine N., Peter O. Wacker and Michael Siegel. *Mapping New Jersey*. New Brunswick, NJ: Rivergate Books, 2009, 122.

Morning Star. "Pilot Uses Up Gas, Then Lands Crippled Plane." September 3, 1941, 3.

Mulvihill, Geoff. "Atlantic City Airport, Where 'Air-port' Coined, Closing." pressofAtlanticCity.com. September 26, 2006. Accessed August 11, 2011.

Omahan World Herald. "Dog Hitch-Hikes 13,512 Miles by Plane from New Guinea, Called 'Choo-Choo.'" January 12, 1945, 4.

———. "Newark Airport Reopens." April 16, 1941, 7.

———. "Newark Field Ruled Unsafe." May 28, 1940, 8.

————. "Planes in Adieu to Newark Field." May 31, 1940, 26.

————. "Plane Strikes Skyscraper." May 21, 1946, 2.

————. "200 War Wounded Evacuated by Air." May 17, 1944, 5.

Oregonian. "Air Schedule Told." January 30, 1946, 8.

Plain Dealer. "Schedules Newark Flights." May 26, 1941, 17.

Repository. "Fog Blamed as Plane Rams Skyscraper." May 21, 1946, 1.

Roddy, Maurice. "America's New Super-Stuka Bomber to Outperform Best Models Abroad." *Dallas Morning News,* October 5, 1941, section VI, 9.

Shapp, Ray. Email correspondence, September 29, 2011.

Springfield Republican. "Airliner Lands Safely." April 13, 1940, 14.

————. "First Air Commuter Now Jests at Cars." July 25, 1941, 2.

————. "Graf Zeppelin May Arrive Four Years to Day after Los Angeles." October 14, 1928, 4.

————. "Permitted to Resume Use of Newark Field." April 10, 1941, 6.

————. "65,000 Pieces of Mail Carried by Zeppelin Bear New Air Stamp." October 14, 1928, 4.

Strunsky, Steve. "Historic Airport Terminal? Yep, and in Newark." *Wired New York,* February 11, 2004. Accessed September 16, 2011.

Times-Picayune. "15 Airplanes Are Sold to Allies by Private Owners." June 2, 1940, 11.

————. "Newark Is Seeking National Air Races." March 1, 1940, 39

————. "Pilot Succeeds with One-Wheel Plane Landing." August 12, 1941, 4.

Trenton Evening Times. "Acts to Thwart Sub Wolf Pack." November 6, 1941, 2.

———. "Airplane Factory at Newark Hangar." February 19, 1940, 3.

———. "Airport Manager Gets Nomination." June 3, 1941, 2.

———. "Cash Lacking, Newark Drops Air Race Plans." April 30, 1940, 10.

———. "Chevalier Named." May 23, 1940, 5.

———. "Democrats Add New Planks; Pascoe Hits Their Platform." June 18, 1946, 1.

———. "Dissention with Mayor Delays Newark Airport." October 14, 1940, 24.

———. "Driscoll Signs Ten Measures." April 3, 1947, 2.

———. "Edge Studies Plans for Newark Airport." July 26, 1946, 6.

———. "Ellenstein Opposes Sale of Airport." September 12, 1946, 6.

———. "Four Are Injured as Plane Crashes." August 8, 1940, 12.

———. "Four Class Three Airports in State." January 3, 1941, 5.

———. "Fund Goes Over Top for Newark Airport." October 16, 1940, 13.

———. "Governor Calls Airport Parlay." May 22, 1940, 11.

———. "Governor Pleads for Newark Port." May 29, 1940, 16.

———. "Great Rivalry Developing Between New York City and New Jersey." January 14, 1940, 8.

———. "Hearing Monday on Port Authority Bills." March 12, 1947, 27.

———. "'Jersey Bounce' Not Like This; Juke Box Causes Spy Scare." July 30, 1942, 1.

———. "Jersey Will Seek More Air Defense." May 15, 1940, 13.

———. "Lack of U.S. Air Program Scored." July 21, 1940, 1, 2.

———. "Mass Flight Over Jersey." August 1, 1947, 1.

———. "Negro Battalion Gets Recognition." July 23, 1940, 4.

———. "Newark Airport Ends Its Career." May 31, 1941, 19.

———. "Newark Airport for Guard Fliers." October 30, 1928, 11.

———. "Newark Airport Is Finally Leased." October 23, 1947, 16.

———. "Newark Airport Resumes Services." June 2, 1941, 10.

———. "Newark Gains Airport Lease." July 11, 1947, 16.

———. "Newark Is Preparing to Close Its Airport." May 14, 1940, 8.

———. "Newark's Airport Nears Collapse." May 27, 1940, 17.

———. "Newark's Decision." October 30, 1947, 14.

———. "New Jersey's Opportunity." August 5, 1946, 8.

———. "New—The Great Silver Fleet Maintains Regular Schedules from Newark Airport" (advertisement). August 6, 1941, 11.

———. "Order for Mobilization of 44th Division Signed by Moore; Troops Report Monday." September 10, 1940, 1.

———. [Photo Page]. September 17, 1941, 13.

———. "Pointed Move to Regain Airport." January 28, 1941, 3.

———. "Port Authority's Newark Airport Offer Is Raised." September 10, 1946, 3.

———. "Report of 2,500 Jobs Attracts 10,000 Persons." February 27, 1940, 11.

———. "Senate Won't Probe Newark Airport Case." March 15, 1940, 30.

———. "76-Million Project Proposed for Development at Newark." August 1, 1946, 7.

———. "$600,00 WPA Cash For Newark Airport." February 11, 1941, 1.

———. "Sloane Demands Speed at Airport." January 3, 1941, 13.

———. "State Will Drop Newark Land Quiz." January 24, 1940, 4.

———. "Superhighway Through Jersey Vital for Defense." November 10, 1940, 1.

———. "Three Air Squadrons Planned for Jersey's National Guard." March 27, 1946, 1.

———. "3 Jersey Residents Are Crash Victims." April 8, 1936, 2.

———. "Throng of 500,000 at Newark Airport." September 15, 1941, 1

———. "Wide Area Is Hit by Dense Fog." December 4, 1941, 2.

———. "Wilentz Declares Probe Absurd." May 15, 1940, 13.

———. "Wilkie Flies North for New York Talk." November 29, 1940, 29.

———. "Youthful Flier Foiled Trying to Take Plane." November 27, 1941, 21.

CHAPTER 7

Anonymous. *History and Proceedings Attending the Presentation of a Medal to Thomas Peterson-Mundy.* Perth Amboy, NJ: H.E. Pickersgill, 1935 (reprint).

———. Manumission Book of Monmouth County, New Jersey, 1791–1844.

———. Marriages Performed by the Pastors of the Second Church of Woodbridge (now the First Presbyterian Church of Metuchen, NJ) 1794 –1857.

———. Record of Black Children 1804–1844.

Chambers, Marcia. "Has 100 Years Made a Difference?" *News Tribune,* March 31, 1970.

Marrin, Richard B. *Runaways of Colonial New Jersey: Indentured Servants, Slaves, Deserters and Prisoners, 1720–1781.* Westminster, MD: Heritage Books, Inc., 2007.

McGinnis, William C. *History of Perth Amboy, New Jersey.* Perth Amboy, NJ: American Publishing Company, 1960.

———. *Thomas Mundy Peterson: First Negro Voter in the United States Under the Fifteenth Amendment to the Constitution.* Perth Amboy, NJ: American Publishing Company, 1960.

New York Times. "Returning Troops." June 11, 1865.

———. "War Meeting in Perth Amboy." August 22, 1862.

Perth Amboy Evening News "The First Colored Voter Dead." February 5, 1904.

———. "He Bought the Medal." February 10, 1904.

———. "Peterson's Medal Is Preserved." February 6, 1904.

———. "Thomas Peterson Buried Saturday." February 8, 1904.

Pickersgill, H.E. "Perth Amboy in History: First Negro Voter." *Perth Amboy Evening News*, December 26, 1923.

About the Author

Gordon Bond is the ePublisher of www.GardenStateLegacy.com, a free online quarterly magazine devoted to New Jersey history. He works as an independent historian, writer and lecturer as well as owning his own graphic design company, Gordon Bond Designs. He published his first book, *James Parker: A Printer on the Eve of Revolution*, in 2010 and is presently working on a book about the Woodbridge train wreck of 1951. A proud native of New Jersey, he lives with his wife, Stephanie M. Hoagland, and their two cats, Daisy and Onslow, in Union Township.

Visit us at
www.historypress.net